ROPING

The Barnes Sports Library

This library of practical sports books covers fundamentals, techniques, coaching and playing hints and equipment for each sport. Leading coaches and players have been selected to write these books, so each volume is authoritative and based upon actual experience. Photographs and drawings, or both, illustrate techniques, equipment and play.

ARCHERY
   by Reichart & Keasey
BAIT CASTING
   by Gilmer Robinson
BASEBALL
   by Daniel E. Jessee
BASKETBALL
   by Charles C. Murphy
BASKETBALL FOR GIRLS
   by Meissner & Meyers
BASKETBALL OFFICIATING
   by Dave Tobey
BETTER BADMINTON
   by Jackson & Swan
BICYCLING
   by Ruth & Raymond Benedict
BOWLING FOR ALL
   by Falcaro & Goodman
BOXING
   by Edwin L. Haislet
CHEERLEADING
   by Loken & Dypwick
FENCING
   by Joseph Vince
FIELD HOCKEY FOR GIRLS
   by Josephine T. Lees
FLY CASTING
   by Gilmer Robinson
FOOTBALL
   by W. Glenn Killinger
FUNDAMENTAL HANDBALL
   by Bernath E. Phillips
GOLF
   by Patty Berg
HOW TO TIE FLIES
   by E. C. Gregg
ICE HOCKEY
   by Edward Jeremiah
JIU-JITSU
   by Frederick P. Lowell
LACROSSE
   by Tad Stanwick
LAWN GAMES
   by John R. Tunis

PADDLE TENNIS
   by Fessenden S. Blanchard
PHYSICAL CONDITIONING
   by Stafford & Duncan
RIDING
   by J. J. Boniface
RIFLE MARKSMANSHIP
   by Lt. Wm. L. Stephens
ROLLER SKATING
   by Bob Martin
ROPING
   by Bernard S. Mason
SIX-MAN FOOTBALL
   by Ray O. Duncan
SKATING
   by Putnam & Parkinson
SKIING
   by Walter Prager
SOCCER AND SPEEDBALL
FOR GIRLS
   by Florence L. Hupprich
SOCCER
   by Samuel Fralick
SOFTBALL
   by Arthur T. Noren
SOFTBALL FOR GIRLS
   by Viola Mitchell
SWIMMING
   by R. J. H. Kiphuth
TABLE TENNIS
   by Jay Purves
TENNIS
   by Helen Jacobs
TENNIS MADE EASY
   by Lloyd Budge
TOUCH FOOTBALL
   by John V. Grombach
TRACK AND FIELD
   by Ray M. Conger
VOLLEY BALL
   by Robert Laveaga
WRESTLING
   by E. C. Gallagher

Clair Bee's Basketball Library

THE SCIENCE OF COACHING :: MAN-TO-MAN DEFENSE AND ATTACK
ZONE DEFENSE AND ATTACK :: DRILLS AND FUNDAMENTALS

ROPING

By

BERNARD S. MASON

A · S · BARNES & COMPANY

NEW YORK

PRINTED IN THE UNITED STATES OF AMERICA

TABLE OF CONTENTS

ROPING

Ropes and Whips

CHAPTER I

Ropes and Roping

I've tried to find the cause of it, but I can't. All I can say is that I'm infected with roping fever, and it is a hopelessly incurable malady. Not that it is unpleasant in its effects or an affliction of which one would want to be relieved—rather the opposite is the truth of the matter, so deliriously happy is one under its spell. But I've been told that it is an unwholesome and pernicious disorder, for it twists the mind in such a way as to cause all things else to seem of trifling importance as compared to making a noose spin and jumping through it. And once you are through it, the most important thing in the world seems to be to get back on the side from which you just came. All of which takes time and energy away from worthwhile things. (At least, so the normal ones say.) But I know that I've got it and can't be cured of it, so I've long since quit trying to stop and just keep trying to rope. And *trying* to rope is the way to put it, for no one can rope perfectly—all he can do is to try and keep trying.

And I know, too, that this roping fever is contagious. For I can name hundreds of people that caught it from me, and are as bad off as I am. And I hope to keep on contaminating folks with it, knowing full well that they will contaminate others. While they may get less work done, they will nevertheless be happier.

However the mind may be affected by it, I am certain on the point that the roping infection has absolutely no injurious physical results. It means work—endless months and years of work. And strenuous work, too, for this matter of twirling the noose of a lariat is vigorous and lusty business. Being gripping and compelling, you drive hard toward your goal of mastery, and quit only when too weary to continue. Now, interesting physical effort never hurt any one—and if exercise is beneficial to the human system, then roping goes down as a bodily tonic *par excellence*, for no one ever roped without getting a workout.

The germ of this whole roping business came from the wild and woolly West of the American plains and mesas. True enough, ropes for catching stock antedate the American West some many years, but the lariat in its present form, and the method of handling it, are a product of those tempestuous, melodramatic days when the West was new and each man a law unto himself. And right here rests perhaps the major reason why roping possesses such an undeniable glamour for boys and men, girls and women—the rope is a symbol of all that rugged and romantic Western picture. And where is there a boy or girl in America whose pulse does not beat a little more rapidly at the thought of those gloriously picturesque days?

But there is something else to roping besides romantic symbols. Minus all this glamour of its early history, it would still compel. Explain it how you will, it gets into the blood and stays there—and this because of something intrinsic in the sport itself. The spinning noose is pleasing to the eye—gracefully floating, rhythmic, circling on and on effortlessly. It makes folks want to be the cause of the spinning themselves. There is an aesthetic something about it.

Furthermore, it is intricate—there is nothing about roping that can be easily picked up. While a few simple tricks may be quickly learned, they but pave the way to the regular feats of the art. If one devotes years to it he will still have much to learn, and will be discontented and impatient with himself for not succeeding more swiftly and fully. I have never known a roping artist of the stage, circus, or rodeo, who felt that he had mastered all there is to roping, and who did not have some other tricks in the back of his mind that he hoped some day to figure out.

The result of all this is that roping is a lifetime task. One never learns it all. Every new wrinkle he learns opens the way to still more wrinkles that he did not know existed before. It challenges and challenges, and refuses to be defeated. This all goes to label roping as a hobby with scarcely an equal. To serve its full function a hobby must be rich enough in content to furnish incentive for a lifetime of effort. This definitely admits roping to the select class. And roping is not one of those quiet intellectual types of hobbies—when one ropes, he not only ropes his way to joy but to health and strength.

You can spin the rope almost any place and any time, and the only equipment needed is your ropes. And you do not need others to help you—it is a one-man sport. You can even practice in the drawing room of your home if you do not have much respect for your furniture, draperies, and the light fixtures! However, it wouldn't be quite advisable to rope in clothes that you expect to use for any other purpose, unless you do not care about the size of your dry-cleaning bill. Ropes have a way of accumulating all the dirt on the lot, and transferring it to clothing or other things that are usually expected to be kept clean.

Enough of the advantages of rope spinning as a sport or a hobby! There is no better exercise, no more compelling and gripping individual sport, no similar play activity quite so filled with intricacies as to challenge one to effort for a lifetime.

Rope spinning, however, can be of no practical importance to the average person, other than for the recreation it supplies. It will never increase his supply of stocks and bonds. Neither has it been of any practical worth to the cowboy of the ranges—in fact, it has often been a detriment to him, for when a perfectly good cow-hand who can rope his steers and catch his calves, begins to learn to spin his noose, the fever infects him to the point where handling stock seems mundane indeed. And to make matters worse, the other cowboys are immediately contaminated by him until loops are whirling all over the place. Now the ranch boss cares not at all for all this spinning business—he wants ropers who can catch the stock and figures on them tending strictly to the business at hand. And if too much time is consumed with Wedding Rings and Butterflies and Ocean Waves, likely as not the boss will issue an order that none of this rope spinning is to be tolerated on the premises. Many a good catch-roper has moved along to seek a new job because of his fancy for spinning nooses.

Of course, the dude ranches today have rope-spinners aplenty, which fact gives the impression that such ropers were always common in the serious life of ranching. But not so—lariat throwing is business, but rope spinning is play.

While rope spinning may have no practical use in itself, lariat throwing is replete with practical applications. Aside from its value in handling stock, it trains a person so that he can manipulate any rope effectively for any purpose. For example, a life line can be handled accurately and efficiently by a boy who can rope without any additional or special practice or training. Life buoys can be tossed more efficiently because of lassoing experience. Knots can be quickly tied and ropes thrown and handled in professional style for sailing or other purposes. The lariat itself can be used in life-saving—there are many instances on record of a drowning person being saved by the noose of a lariat being thrown over his struggling body—and this is more pleasant and certain of results than diving into the water after him. Sportsmen sometimes use their lariats in hunting—mountain lions and even polar bears have been captured by means of nothing more formidable than a lass-rope.

It should be apparent by this time that rope spinning is one thing and catch-roping is something else. The equipment is different and the movements have little in common. A head-line catch-roper might be entirely helpless with a spinning rope, and similarly, a stage rope-spinner might not be able to rope a calf if his life depended on it. There is one respect in which the two arts are interwoven—the so-called trick-and-fancy roping of the circuses and rodeos involves catching horses after a preliminary display of rope spinning. The roper spins his lariat in an Ocean Wave, jumps through it a time or two as the horse approaches, and then ropes him without stopping the spinning noose. While the two arts must be regarded as separate, yet they are similar enough in nature to go hand in hand for recreational purposes, and people interested in learning one would certainly want to know something of the other.

Ancient as the catch-rope is, rope spinning is a new wrinkle.

It was a Mexican named Vincenti Orespo who first displayed a spinning loop in this country. This was shortly before the turn of the century, and he was signed up forthwith by Buffalo Bill for his Wild West show. Orespo was a crack catch-roper but did only a few spins, which latter were sufficient, however, to claim for him the honor of originating modern rope spinning. This Mexican would be amazed today, could he see the intricacies of the modern roper's art, for the American cowboys were not slow in taking to this sport, once they got the idea.

I can wish you no greater joy than that which will result if the roping fever catches you. And I hope these pages may be the cause of your catching it and spreading it among others.

So good luck, and good roping!

PLACE IN THE SCHOOL AND RECREATIONAL PROGRAM

Any vigorous and compelling activity of the type that is apt to carry on as recreation· and beneficial exercise throughout life has a place in a school's physical education program. Similarly, any wholesome activity that brings joy at the moment and, once the skills have been developed, gives promise of continuing to bring joy in the future, has a place in a recreational program. That roping possesses these qualifications to the majority of those who have come to know it has already been indicated—it grips and compels peculiarly. Its fascination seems never to wane. It possesses such endless variations that one never masters them all— it challenges throughout life. In short, roping instruction constitutes excellent education for leisure.

At the time it is being learned, and as long as it is practiced, roping is better exercise than the average gymnasium and playground activity in which one can engage alone and without playmates. It fills the need for strenuous physical activity. The desire for mastery is there, always serving as a driving force to vigorous effort, yet complete mastery seems never to be achieved. As a beneficial physical exercise, roping has much to recommend it.

Rope spinning is of particular interest in the field of correctives.

It is ideal exercise for that group of individuals who because of physical handicaps cannot wisely enter whole-heartedly into the team games of the average student. It can be participated in as strenuously or as leisurely as the individual desires, and can be enjoyed whether alone or in the presence of companions. The compelling interest it develops leads to practice at home as well as in the gymnasium. Roping tricks may be selected that furnish desirable exercise for the improvement of most posture mal-adjustments.

With all its other attributes which recommend it to physical education and recreation, roping has that priceless asset, *appeal to the imagination*. It brings delight beyond and above that which comes from performing a vigorous and difficult feat. It takes the roper in imagination to those romantic days of the old West that the rope invariably symbolizes.

Not only is the roper's imagination stimulated in these ways, but the spectators are similarly inspired. This being the case, roping serves admirably as a feature for exhibitions and demonstrations in the physical education and recreation program. Few spots on the program will carry so much glamour as will a dozen or more rope spinners on the floor or field, all spinning their ropes in colorful and intricate fashion. Roping can be worked into demonstrations, pageants, and dancing exhibitions in many and intriguing ways.

Roping falls in line with the present-day trend in physical education to include new and colorful activities that have strong imaginative appeal. Few activities will have as strong a romantic touch and at the same time be as beneficial from the standpoint of wholesome exercise.

PARTS OF A ROPE

First off, let us familiarize ourselves with the parts of a lariat and the terms applied to the various sections of a spinning rope and catch-rope.

A rope used in catching animals is variously called a lariat, riata, lass-rope, catch-rope, or soga, but those who use it regularly are inclined to call it just a rope. The term "lariat" is seldom applied to a spinning rope—men who handle both types refer to one as a spinning rope and the other as a catch-rope. "Lasso," coming from the Spanish *lazo*, is seldom used as the name for a rope—it is more commonly used as a verb referring to the act of throwing a lariat. The word "lariat" is derived from the Spanish "la riata."

Both the spinning rope and the catch-rope, although made of different materials, are constructed according to the same prin-

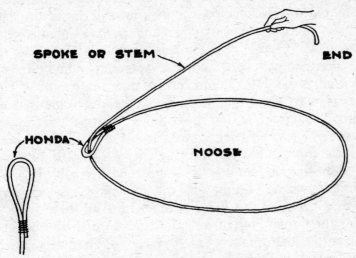

SPOKE OR STEM

END

HONDA

NOOSE

FIGURE 1. PARTS OF A SPINNING ROPE

ciple. One end of the rope is doubled back to form a small loop or eye about two inches long—this is called a *honda* (see Figure 1). When the other end of the rope is passed through this honda, as in Figure 1, the large loop thus formed is called a *loop* or *noose*, and the section from the honda to the end is called the *stem* or *spoke*.

THE SPINNING ROPE

Practically every boy and man has tried at some time to learn to spin a rope. And the handiest rope being the ever-present clothesline, it was usually pressed into service as a spinning rope. But the clothesline refused to spin! There is nothing unusual about this, for a clothesline would refuse to function in the hands of even the most expert of ropers. Often a ready-made lariat of the type designed for roping steers is secured from a western supply store by the aspiring rope-spinner. It, too, refuses to spin —and rightly so, for it is not made for spinning.

There is nothing more certain than the fact that one will never learn to spin a rope unless he has a rope suitable for the purpose. Just any old rope one happens to pick up will not fit the bill and will very probably mean defeat and perhaps permanent discouragement. Herein rests the reason why so many have found their experience with rope spinning unpleasant and why they have given it up as too difficult and forbidding. Frequently I worked for weeks in my struggling, learning days, endeavoring to master a certain trick, only to find in the end that the rope I was using was not just right for this trick. No matter how faithfully one may follow the instructions given in the chapters that follow, success will not smile upon him if he is using a rope unsuitable in material, length, and weight. So the first rule in roping is, *secure just the right rope for the trick being practiced*. And there is no need of using the wrong kind of rope, for the best of rope for spinning can be purchased for a very small sum at any hardware store.

Ordinary Manilla rope is useless for rope spinning. A good roper may be able to make it spin, but he certainly cannot do many tricks with it. Both for learning purposes and for expert performance, it is out of the question.

The rope that is needed is *braided cotton sash cord, three-eighths inch in thickness*. Of the several qualities of sash cord, the best type of *spot lariat cord* is required—the name "spot cord" is commonly given this rope because of the colored spots it contains. There are two qualities of this cord, one called *spot cord* and the other *spot lariat cord*, the latter being a harder braid manufactured especially for spinning which does not loosen up and become softened with use. Either of these cords will answer the purpose well for the average roper. Most of the larger hardware stores carry spot cord of the quality needed. Be sure to secure the three-eighths-inch thickness—this is commonly called Number 12.

The length of the rope depends upon the trick we are trying to learn or do. The flat spins described in the next chapter, which are the tricks that the beginner should learn first, require a twenty-foot rope and a fourteen-foot rope. If only one rope can be afforded, it should be twenty feet long.

Made-up spinning ropes may be purchased at a cost very slightly in excess of the cost of the rope required for making them, but there is really no need of buying a ready-made rope in that any one can prepare the rope for spinning in ten minutes.

First, it is necessary to make the honda.

MAKING THE HONDA

Double one end of the rope back, making an eye or loop, the opening of which is about two inches long. Make the loop secure by wiring it tightly with medium-weight copper wire, as illustrated in A, Figure 2. Three to six strands of wire should be sufficient to hold it—more wire may make the honda too heavy. Now wrap a strand or two of wire or a little adhesive tape around the other end of the rope to keep it from unraveling. Insert the straight end through the honda and the rope is complete and ready to use.

Many ropers prefer to use the rope without protecting the end against unraveling until it has unraveled four or five inches. They then wire it to prevent further unraveling. This produces an unraveled tassel at the end of the rope that has a nice appearance and in no way detracts from the rope's usefulness.

Some roping artists desire to protect the end of the honda from wear and so wrap it with copper wire as shown in B, Figure 2, or sew a piece of leather around it as in C. Such hondas are also often used when it is desired to give the rope a little additional weight for certain tricks. The average roper will find no use for such protected hondas, however, and certainly they should be avoided by beginners. The ideal honda is shown in A, Figure 2.

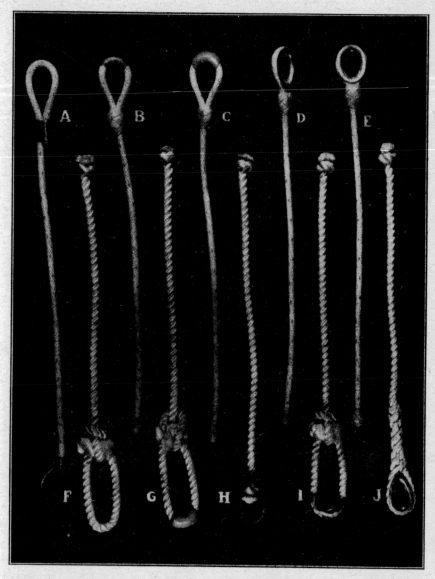

FIGURE 2. VARIOUS TYPES OF HONDAS: *A to E, Spinning Rope Hondas:* A, plain light honda; B, same with end wrapped with wire; C, same with end wrapped with leather; D, aluminum honda; E, brass honda. *F to J, Catch-rope Hondas:* F, standard honda made with lariat-loop knot; G, same with end wrapped with leather; H, rawhide honda; I, Hogue's Honda or brass half-honda; J, standard brass honda, spliced.

All hondas prepared by Hamley & Co., Pendleton, Oregon.

The hondas shown in B and C have the wiring covered with a plait of leather. Pleasing as this is to the eye, it should be avoided for the reason that it adds weight that is a hindrance in the tricks for which these light-honda ropes are used.

METAL HONDAS

Some ropers prefer to use the light aluminum honda illustrated in D, Figure 2. These are so light that they add very little weight to the honda, but there is really no purpose in using them. In fact, they make more difficult the performing of most roping tricks and certainly should not be used by beginners. When one develops skill and can do many tricks, he will possess several ropes and may then want one equipped with an aluminum honda which he may find useful for certain stunts. But this must be determined by experience—on the start, use the simple, unweighted honda described in the preceding section and do not attempt to use the aluminum type until you have learned all the fine points of the roping game. And even then, you probably will find no place for it.

The heavy brass honda illustrated in E, Figure 2, however, is used regularly in rope spinning, but only in the more advanced tricks which require a heavily weighted rope. In the hands of a beginner learning the flat spins, one of these heavy hondas would render the rope useless. It is used chiefly in the vertical spins described in Chapter III, and here it is indispensable. Do not attempt to use one until you are ready to learn these difficult vertical spins. The finest of ropers could not do the flat spins successfully with a brass honda, and the flat spins are the tricks with which a beginner must start.

Brass hondas for spinning ropes may be purchased at very small cost from any manufacturer of spinning ropes or any western cowboy outfitter. Wrap the end of the rope around the honda and wire the end to the standing part of the rope very tightly with copper wire. With such a heavy honda, the wiring may be covered with leather if desired, as shown in C, Figure 2. Some ropers prefer to sew the end to the standing part with heavy linen thread instead of wiring it, but this makes a delicate rope that is not suitable for any one except an expert who handles his rope skillfully and gently. A beginner, of necessity, subjects his rope to hard usage because of his lack of skill in handling it, and consequently the honda should be wired in place. Wired hondas are used by ninety-nine out of every hundred ropers anyway.

THE THROWING LARIAT

While there is only one kind of rope usable for rope spinning, there are many kinds of ropes that do service in lassoing. And which of these is best depends upon the purpose for which it is to be used. Actual roping of steers and horses on the range calls for one kind of rope; trick-and-fancy catching in the circuses demands another type; learning to throw a lariat requires still another. And since these pages are designed for those who are learning the skills of the lariat, we shall consider first the practice rope, and then discuss each of the other types in turn.

MAKING A PRACTICE ROPE

In learning to throw a lariat there is no better rope than ordinary three-eighths-inch Manilla rope obtainable at any hardware store. It serves better than the special hemp lariat rope from which the catch-ropes of the ranches are made, in that the latter are too heavy and stiff for the beginner to handle easily. Once the knack has been mastered with an ordinary Manilla rope, the regular lariats can be easily and skillfully manipulated.

Secure thirty-five feet of three-eighths-inch Manilla rope. The honda may be made in several ways: The easiest, quickest, and best way is to tie the lariat-loop illustrated in Figure 3. This is the method commonly used on the plains in making a temporary lariat out of rope. Simply tie an overhand knot about ten inches from the end of the rope, leaving it loose as illustrated in A, Figure 3. Then tuck the end through the knot following the course indicated by the arrow. Tie an ordinary overhand knot with this end to prevent it from pulling out, then jam the whole knot as tightly as possible. The honda then appears as in B, Figure 3. The lariat-loop makes a nicely shaped honda that stays open all the time, and the weight of the knot gives the Manilla rope just the right amount of weight to enable it to be easily handled. The hondas shown in F, G, and I, Figure 2, are made in this way.

Hondas may also be made by wiring the end to the standing part as in making the honda on a spinning rope (A, Figure 2),

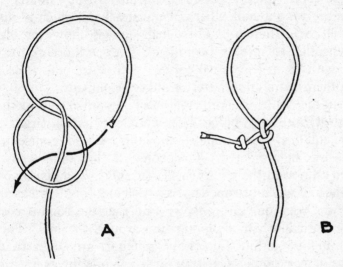

FIGURE 3. HOW THE LARIAT-LOOP IS TIED

or by splicing the end into the standing part with an eye-splice. Splicing makes an excellent honda but for some reason was seldom used in making lariats on the ranches. Wiring does not make nearly as strong a honda on a catch-rope as does the lariat-loop.

Never use metal hondas on a practice rope. Occasionally the catch-ropes of the ranches have a small brass honda such as shown in J, Figure 2, but such hondas weight the rope too much for practice purposes. Furthermore, they are dangerous: it would be very easy to injure a person by throwing at him a lariat equipped with one of these brass weights, and many a horse has had an eye knocked out by them.

If it seems necessary to weight the honda slightly so that the noose will carry better or to protect it from wear when thrown, wrap the end half of the honda with copper wire of the medium-heavy size, or cover it with leather as illustrated in G, Figure 2.

Another device often used on the ranges is the metal half-honda shown in I, Figure 2. This is a curved piece of brass which is slipped inside the end of the honda loop and hammered tightly onto the rope. Such a device is called a Hogue's honda. It increases the weight somewhat but not nearly so much as does the full-sized brass honda. These half-hondas, however, are not recommended for use by beginners. Those who desire to equip lariats with them for actual service with cattle and horses may obtain them from any western saddlery company.

When the honda is completed, insert the other end of the rope through it, and the rope has been converted into a lariat. With use, the end of the rope opposite the honda will, of course, unravel and needs to be protected. To accomplish this, many a cow-hand has tied a knot on the end of his lariat and this to his sorrow, for came the day when he roped a frisky colt and found it necessary to release the rope quickly, only to find that the rope persisted in staying with him and dragging him around the lot. The knot caught in his clothing somehow, as knots are wont to do, or perhaps on the saddle or its trappings. While the average person just learning to rope will not be throwing at temperamental colts, yet as a matter of principle, the end of the rope should be wrapped with a strand or two of wire so that it will slip out of the hand quickly and freely whenever it is given a sudden jerk.

CATCH-ROPES

The catch-ropes used in the work-a-day life of the cowboys are usually made of an extra quality hemp rope that is exceptionally smooth and hard in finish. Some of these ropes are specially treated so that they are not affected by atmospheric changes and can be handled as easily in damp weather as in dry. This is important to cowboys in that ordinary Manilla rope becomes stiff and kinky when damp, and is often limp and lifeless after it has been dried out. Made-up catch-ropes of these types, and rope in bulk for the making of lariats, may be secured from any western saddlery company or cowboy outfitting concern. Such ropes are essential for actual roping of steers and horses, but as stated in the preceding section, are not as desirable as ordinary cheap Manilla rope in the hands of a beginner who is just starting to learn the art.

Professional catch-ropes come in several sizes. For roping calves, the three-eighths inch scant or the three-eighths inch full size is preferred. For small stock, the seven-sixteenths-inch scant size makes a good all-around rope. Steer and horse roping calls for the seven-sixteenths-inch full size or the half-inch size, which latter will stand any emergency that can arise in roping, but is too heavy to handle conveniently and is usually utilized only when extra heavy strain is anticipated. The average catch-rope is seven-sixteenths inch in diameter.

Catch-ropes vary in length from thirty-five to fifty feet. Forty feet is about the right length for normal conditions.

In regard to hondas on catch-ropes, four types are in common use. The lariat-loop described in the preceding section, (Figure 3) is often seen, but is almost always covered with leather to protect the rope, the leather being wrapped around the rope in the honda loop and sewed along the outside edge as illustrated in G, Figure 2. The brass honda is occasionally utilized but only on heavy ropes and under conditions where the lariat must be thrown long distances. Its use is limited to steers almost entirely, it being seldom desirable in handling horses. The metal half-honda illustrated in I, Figure 2, is not common, but is preferable to the full-sized brass honda in that it furnishes sufficient weight and protection for ordinary conditions, yet does not offer such a great hazard to animals. Still another honda often used on catch-ropes is the rawhide honda, shown in H, Figure 2. It consists of an eye of heavy rawhide attached to the rope in such a way as to enable it to revolve. This honda is light and serviceable, and entirely harmless to any living creatures that it may hit. Such rawhide hondas can be secured from any western cowboy out-fitter.

While each of these special types of hondas has its use in the work of the cowboys, they are scarcely necessary when the lariat is used for recreational purposes. Here, a lariat-loop is all that is needed; it may be wrapped with leather or wound with copper wire if it is to be subjected to an unusual amount of use.

THE MAGUEY ROPE

The maguey lariat is the rope used by all the professionals of the circuses, rodeos, and vaudeville stage for trick-and-fancy catches. It is the finest of all ropes for expert trick roping but is not recommended for regular lariat purposes in handling stock on the ranges.

The maguey rope is made by hand in Old Mexico from agave fiber. It is a handsome rope with a very smooth and hard finish, and as contrasted to the Manilla ropes, it never becomes raggy and soft with use. Because of its unusually hard surface and firm nature it permits a more finished performance and holds a loop better than any other lariat made. Furthermore, it can be thrown with greater precision and accuracy than regular lariat ropes. The trick-and-fancy roping acts of the circuses and rodeos involve both rope spinning and trick catching. The maguey rope spins beautifully for the vertical spinning tricks used in these maneuvers, and at the same time is the finest of catch-ropes.

The maguey rope is thoroughly to be recommended to every one interested in learning to handle a catch-rope accurately. However, it is not the rope with which a beginner should receive his first initiation into the art of roping. Its stiffness will prove confusing to him until after he has used an ordinary Manilla rope for a while.

The maguey rope has one rather serious shortcoming for every one except an expert, and one that often proves distracting even to the professionals: in damp weather it becomes exceedingly stiff and wiry. To guard against this, it is well to keep the rope in a warm place when the weather is damp, taking it out only when needed.

Since the maguey rope is a four-strand rope, a special type of honda is used on it. Run a marline spike through the rope twelve inches from the end, thus separating the rope with two strands on each side of the spike. Through this opening force the end of

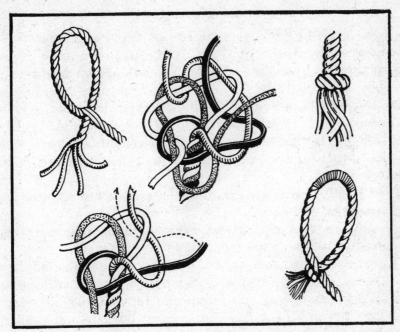

FIGURE 4. HONDA FOR A FOUR-STRAND MAGUEY ROPE, USING THE TUCKED WALL KNOT

the rope, making a loop two-and-one-half inches long as shown in Figure 4. Then unravel the strands of the end and tie a tucked wall knot, following the method clearly shown in Figure 4. The honda may be wrapped with a little copper wire at the end, or may be covered with leather. There are other more complicated methods of making a honda on a maguey rope, but the one described above is the more common and answers every purpose.

Maguey ropes are remarkably inexpensive considering their fine quality. They may be obtained from any western saddlery or cowboy outfitting company for less money than good hemp catch-ropes will cost. They range in length from thirty-five to fifty feet, the smaller sizes running about three-eighths of an inch thick. By specifying a professional grade of maguey rope, an extra long and large size may be obtained. Since maguey ropes are hand-made, they vary a great deal in size and workmanship.

HORSEHAIR ROPES

Ropes made of horsehair appear to be as old as the history of the horse in the American West. They have been made by the Indians and Mexicans for centuries and were much used by the cowboys of the early days. They were not uncommon in Europe also, and are said to be used today by peasants in various regions of France. Although they are still made by Mexicans and Indians, the hair rope has given way almost completely in America to the modern hemp rope which is by all odds a more efficient roping tool.

The hair rope has many shortcomings. It is often a little too light to serve well as a catch-rope, it being difficult to throw it far enough to make long catches. With use it becomes raggy and rough, and at all times has a tendency toward kinking.

Certainly the hair rope served well its purpose in the old days, but the modern riatas have relegated it largely to the curio stores and Wild West shows. Mexican- and Indian-made hair ropes, however, are still for sale at most western cowboy and saddlery outfitters, and are an interesting novelty to add to a roper's collection of lariats.

THE RAWHIDE LARIAT

As is the case with the hair ropes, the rawhide lariats belong largely to yesterday. They were the standard and almost universally used rope for hard use in the early days of the West, but today have been supplanted by modern hemp ropes not only because of the labor and time required in making rawhide sogas, but because of the greater efficiency of the hemp lass-rope.

As compared to the modern hemp ropes, rawhide riatas are

heavier and more unwieldy, and do not retain a loop as well. Then, too, while they are unusually strong and tough throughout the most of their lengths, they often have a weak spot which will give way at the time when strength and dependability are most needed. Once a strand is broken the entire rope is rendered useless.

In the old days the rawhide ropes were made from buffalo hide, or from buck or elk. Buck hide is still used by the Indians today and makes an especially fine rope. In making the rope, the hide is cut into one long strand about a half inch wide by going round and round the hide. Four strands are braided together by hand into the rope. The making of a good rope is a long and tedious process requiring endless hours of rolling and pounding to make it even and round, not to speak of the boiling and greasing to waterproof and soften it.

Like the hair ropes, the rawhide lariats belong largely to the Wild West shows and the western curio stores, although they are still made by the Mexicans and can be purchased through western cowboy outfitters.

CARING FOR A LARIAT

Every rope must be broken in before it will work effectively. New rope is stiff and full of kinks as a rule. The perennial method of conditioning a rope in the West is to tie it on behind a wagon, or to the saddle, and thus let it drag for a half a day on the ground. Another method commonly used is to lay it over a post and pull it back and forth strenuously with the hands. Braided cotton rope used for rope spinning does not require this kind of breaking in— a half hour of use will properly loosen up such a rope. However, in initiating new hemp and maguey ropes much time will be saved if they are conditioned by one of the two methods described above.

Once the rope has been broken in and is adjusted so that the roper can use it himself for the tricks that he does, he will want to take particular care of it and use it only for this purpose. Otherwise it will soon become unbalanced and inefficient. Every professional roper guards his ropes with great caution and does not permit any one else to use them. Spinning ropes particularly are temperamental affairs, each one seeming to have an individuality of its own. To use a spinning rope as a lariat and throw it at some one is to abuse it in a way that no spinning rope should be treated. Use the spinning rope as a spinning rope only and do not allow other people to handle it. Once you get a good rope that will do intricate tricks for you, you may try a long time to find another that will do these stunts as well. A roper invariably becomes attached to his ropes and it usually happens that the oldest and least attractive of the ropes is the one that the roping artist prizes the most.

Dampness is not good for any rope. Untreated hemp rope becomes limp and lifeless as compared to its condition before wetting. Even though the better quality of catch-ropes are specially treated with water-proofing, yet they should not be subjected to undue dampness. Maguey ropes are so susceptible to dampness that they are not a practical rope in sections of the country where the climate is consistently damp. When there is dampness in the air, they become exceedingly stiff and wiry, but when dried out, show fewer ill effects than most other ropes. A wet spinning rope is extremely difficult to handle.

A spinning rope can be washed in soap and water when it gets dirty. Cotton ropes pick up so much dirt, and soil everything they touch to such an extent, that they should be cleaned often. The washing does not damage them at all.

Always coil your ropes carefully when you are through using them and hang them up or store them away in a dry place.

CHAPTER II

Rope Spinning—The Flat Spins

While catch-roping involves the throwing of a lariat in such a way that the noose encircles and tightens on an animal or other object, rope spinning consists of manipulating a short rope in such a way that the loop becomes dilated and remains open in circular form as long as it is revolved. This loop is swung around the body of the roper in various tricks and stunts. When the loop is revolving the centrifugal force keeps it open so that it remains dilated and in circular form in the air. The friction of the honda against the spoke prevents the noose from collapsing.

The various rope-spinning tricks are of two general types, the *flat spins* and the *vertical spins*. In the flat spins, the loop spins in a horizontal plane, that is, parallel to the ground, whereas in the vertical spins, the loop revolves in a vertical plane, perpendicular to the floor. The flat spins are much easier to learn and do than are the vertical tricks, and certainly must be learned first. This chapter describes the flat spins—the vertical maneuvers are presented in the chapter following.

There are two fundamental flat spins which are the basis of all the tricks in flat roping. These are called the *Wedding Ring* and the *Flat Loop*. The difference lies in the fact that in the Wedding Ring the roper stands *inside* the spinning loop, whereas in the Flat Loop, he stands outside the loop and spins it in front of his body or manipulates it around himself. Both of these tricks are very simple and easy to learn—they are the first tricks to be undertaken, being basic to the more intricate maneuvers.

There is a number of tricks based on the Wedding Ring, and these are presented in the pages that follow under the heading, The Wedding-Ring Series. Similarly, there is a number of stunts based on the Flat Loop which are presented under the heading, The Flat-Loop Series. Then there are several tricks combining the Wedding Ring and the Flat Loop—these are described under the heading, The Combination Series.

As stated in the preceding chapter, braided cotton sash cord is the only rope usable for rope spinning. This is commonly called spot cord (see page 8).

GRADED LIST OF FLAT SPINS

Roping tricks vary a great deal in complexity and difficulty. They build up one upon another, the skills learned in one opening the way to the learning of another, which latter would be much more difficult were it not for the ability developed in the preceding. To attempt too difficult a trick before the proper foundation has been laid will probably result in failure and perhaps permanent discouragement.

The following list indicates the recommended order in which the tricks should be learned:

1. Flat Loop
2. Wedding Ring
3. Hand-shaking
4. Hand-shaking around One Leg
5. Lying Down
6. Jumping into the Flat Loop
7. Jumping Out
8. Up and Over
9. Merry-go-round
10. Two-handed Merry-go-round
11. Tapping In and Out
12. Juggling
13. The Bounce
14. Juggling Up and Over
15. Hand-shaking around Alternate Legs
16. Hurdling
17. The Big Loop
18. Lift onto Body
19. Lift onto Arm
20. The Skyrocket
21. Spinning Two Ropes

THE TWO FUNDAMENTAL SPINS

The two fundamental spins in flat roping are the *Flat Loop* and the *Wedding Ring*. Once these two spins are perfected so that they can be performed easily and without conscious effort, the road is wide open to all the spectacular tricks that involve a

flat loop. Without perfection in these two fundamentals, however, the others are impossible.

THE FLAT LOOP

Rope—fourteen feet long with a light honda.

In the Flat Loop a small loop is spun in front of the body so
that the plane of the loop is parallel to the ground, as illustrated
in Figure 5. This is the simplest of all tricks and the easiest
to learn, and, although not as fascinating as the Wedding Ring,
it is the trick that should be learned first in most cases.

Use a fourteen-foot length of Number 12 spot lariat cord

FIGURE 5. SPINNING THE FLAT LOOP

with a light honda (see page 9). While this trick can be
done with a rope of any length, the ideal length for learning is
fourteen feet. Arrange the rope as shown in A, Figure 5. The
roper in this picture is using a longer rope and consequently the
end extends over into his left hand—if a fourteen-foot length
were used the right hand would grip the spoke at its very end.
The reason why a fourteen-foot rope is preferred in learning
is because we are not troubled with this long end extending over
into the left hand.

Note that the spoke goes straight through the honda and is

not doubled back—Figure 6 shows the right way and the wrong way to arrange the rope preliminary to spinning.

In arranging the rope as in A, Figure 5, the end of the rope is held between the thumb and forefinger of the right hand, the other fingers of the right hand being used to hold the loop. The left hand merely holds the loop open. Note that the spoke ex-

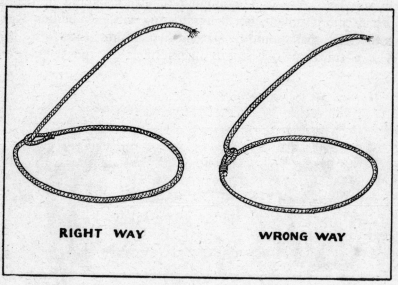

RIGHT WAY   **WRONG WAY**

FIGURE 6. RIGHT AND WRONG WAY TO ARRANGE THE NOOSE

tends from the hand nearly down to the floor—the correct length for the spoke is about one half the diameter of the loop. Note also that the roper is leaning slightly forward at the hips with his hands well below the level of the waist.

With everything all arranged as in A, Figure 5, we are ready to spin the loop. Keeping the left hand just where it is, throw the loop over to the left with the right hand. Do this a few times without attempting to spin it. Then throw it over to the left as before and, as you do so, release the rope with the left hand and give it a circular spin from right to left (counterclockwise) with the right hand, releasing the loop with the right hand and keeping hold of the end of the spoke only.

There is no magic in rope spinning—the rope will not spin of its own accord and you must actually give it its initial spin in such a way as to start it spinning. In starting the spin, the right hand must cut a *circle* in the air of approximately the same size that the spinning noose is to be. *Do not release the loop with the right hand too soon*—you should retain hold of the loop until the hand has cut almost a complete circle in the air. Then release it and keep it going by means of the spoke held in the right hand. After making the initial spin of the size of the loop, raise the right hand slightly, and continue to cut circles in the air with it, each circle being a little smaller than the preceding, until the arm at last becomes stationary, the rope being spun with a gentle wrist motion. In making each succeeding circle smaller, the hand follows a spiral course as shown in Figure 7.

FIGURE 7.

In giving the loop its initial spin, it is as if the wheel of a bicycle lying on the ground were being turned—the hand would grasp the tire and would of necessity make a circular movement around the circumference of the wheel. Before releasing the loop, the hand must make just such a circular movement of about the same size as the loop.

Care should be taken not to throw the rope away in giving it the initial spin—the arm should move very slowly, more slowly than the speed necessary to spin the rope once it is going. After releasing the loop, increase the speed steadily but be careful not to jerk it. Once you get the loop spinning, *take it easy*—relax and spin it gently and slowly. It is a wrist rather than an arm motion. Every beginner wants to spin the loop rapidly, using a vigorous arm motion. This not only tends to collapse the loop but produces a choppy motion of the rope that is unattractive to the eye. Most of the failure during your learning days will be due to jerky arm movements resulting from overanxiety and the use of too much muscle.

Rope spinning is *rhythm*. Once the loop is spinning, keep it going in perfect time. Counting as you spin will help to keep the rhythm constant, but with experience this will be unnecessary in that you will be able to feel the rhythm of the rope as the spoke passes a certain spot. If the rhythm is to be increased or decreased, the change must be made very slowly and gradually. The most graceful spinning loops result from a rather slow and gentle motion.

Preventing the Spoke from Twisting.—The spinning of the loop naturally twists the spoke and unless definite precautions are taken the rope will become so twisted and kinky in a moment or two that it will refuse to spin. To guard against this, grip the end very gently and allow it to turn in the hand as it chooses. If you open the hand for a fraction of a second each spin, the spoke will turn of its own accord. Or you may find it easier to turn the spoke with your fingers with each revolution of the loop.

If the rope becomes twisted it is a waste of time to try to spin it—stop the spinning and untwist it before continuing. Never try to straighten out a kinked rope by stepping on it and pulling—untwist it by swinging it in the air in the opposite direction to that used in spinning.

Increasing the Size of the Loop.—All that is necessary to increase the size of the loop is to increase the speed of the spinning. This tends to throw the honda up nearer the hand and shorten the spoke. If there be some excess rope extending over into the left hand, increase the speed of the spinning and, as you do so, open the spinning hand and let some of the excess rope slip out. In this way the loop can be increased to the extent of the rope.

Decreasing the Size of the Loop.—Decreasing the size of the loop is not quite so easy as increasing it. Slow down the speed of the spinning, lower the spinning hand a little, and then jerk it back up to its original position again. The loop will become smaller and the spoke proportionately longer.

If you wish to decrease the size of the loop and also shorten the spoke, slow down the speed of the spinning, slip the spinning hand down a few inches toward the honda, thus shortening the spoke, and then increase the spinning to the normal speed again.

Spinning with the Left Hand.—Having mastered the Flat Loop with the right hand, the next move should be to spin it with the left hand. The mark of a finished performer in any kind of roping is the ability to work as efficiently with his left hand as with his right.

The quickest way to learn left-handed spinning is to start the Flat Loop as usual with the right hand, and when it is going nicely, transfer the spoke from the right to the left hand, and then keep it going with the left hand. Once the left hand has acquired the "feel" of the spinning noose, it is no problem at all to start the spin from the beginning with the left hand. Preliminary to spinning, the loop is held just as in A, Figure 5, except that the hands are crossed: the left hand reaches over and holds the end of the spoke and loop in the position of the right hand in Figure 5, and the right arm crosses under the left and holds the loop open in the position of the left hand in Figure 5.

The Clockwise Flat Spin.—In the Flat Loop as described above, the loop is spun in a counterclockwise direction—this is the standard type of spin and the direction in which the rope is revolved ninety-nine per cent of the time in all rope spinning. However, the beginner should learn to spin each trick in the opposite or clockwise direction as he goes along. After the counterclockwise spin has been mastered, it is but a task of a few minutes to learn to spin the loop in the opposite direction.

Arrange the loop as in A, Figure 5. Then reverse the position of the loop, turning it over so that the arms are crossed, the right hand as it holds the end of the spoke being in front of the left leg, and the left arm crossing behind the right with the left hand in front of the right leg. From this position proceed to spin it in a clockwise direction. It will be easy if you have already learned the standard Flat Loop.

Clockwise Spin with Left Hand.—When spinning with the right hand the counterclockwise spin is the normal and natural movement, whereas with the left hand, the clockwise spin is the natural spin. Arrange rope as in A, Figure 5, except that the sides are reversed, the left hand holding the end of the spoke. Proceed exactly as described above for the standard Flat Loop except that all movements described for the right hand are performed with the left and the direction of the spin is reversed.

THE WEDDING RING

Rope—twenty feet long with a light honda.

Simple though it be, there is no more attractive and appealing trick in roping than the Wedding Ring. When properly done it is graceful and beautiful indeed.

FIGURE 8.   THE WEDDING RING

And happily, it is one of the easiest tricks to master—many even feel that it should be learned before the simple Flat Loop is undertaken. The Wedding Ring is a flat loop inside of which the roper stands and which he spins around his body as illustrated in Figure 8. It is sometimes called the Crinoline or the Body Spin.

The Wedding Ring calls for a twenty-foot rope. Arrange the rope exactly as shown in A, Figure 9. Note that the end of the spoke is held in the right hand and that the honda is about at the level of the ground—this produces a spoke of just the right length regardless of the height of the roper. Note also that the left hand merely holds the loop open.

Keeping the left hand at the level of the waist, pick up the loop with the right hand and turn it back over the head as shown in B, Figure 9. Let it fall around the body and drop to the level of the waist as in C, Figure 9. Move slowly and deliberately in turning the rope back over the head, *and be sure to keep the left hand low.* Every beginner is inclined to raise the left hand, thus throwing the rope wildly behind the back. Make this movement several times before attempting to start the spin.

When the rope has dropped to the level of the waist, as in C, Figure 9, give the noose a hard spin *around* the body from right to left with both hands as indicated by the arrow—be sure that

FIGURE 9. STARTING THE WEDDING RING

the motion of the hands is a *circular* one around the body. As you do so, release the loop with both hands retaining hold of the end of the spoke only, and raise the right hand around behind the head and then up over the head, keeping it going with a gentle motion of the wrist. Figure 10 shows the finished trick.

Two things you must watch, for your failure in starting the spin will probably be due to one of these factors: do not raise the left hand as you toss the rope back over the head with the right hand, and secondly, do not use too much muscle in lifting the rope with the right hand. Either of these mistakes will throw the rope away. Take the starting movements very slowly and gently and give the loop plenty of time to settle down to the level of the waist. In learning, one naturally is over-anxious and tense, and as a result he uses too much muscle and hurries too much. *Relax and take it easy*.

Once the rope is spinning, keep the right hand directly over

FIGURE 10. THE COMPLETED WEDDING RING

the top of the head and spin with the wrist. Whatever you do, guard against a wide swinging motion of the arm. Keep the wrist relaxed and flexible. Try to guide the rope with the thumb and forefinger of the right hand—it is such a delicate and gentle movement that the thumb and finger are all that are needed. Sway the body gently, almost imperceptibly, with the rhythm of the spinning noose—this in itself is enough to keep the spin going, thus relieving the wrist of any important part in the process, once the spin is under way. The tendency always is to speed up the spin and to use the arm to accomplish it; this results in a choppy motion that hurls the noose against the body. If the loop hits the body while being spun gently, the chances are that you are not keeping your right hand directly over your head—if the rope touches you in front, move the hand farther forward, whereas if it touches you behind, move the hand back.

Try to spin as smoothly and gracefully as possible. A slowly spinning, floating loop is always the goal in good roping.

As in all roping tricks, the Wedding Ring must be spun with perfect rhythm. It is well to count during the beginning days, saying *one* and, *two* and, etc., as the loop rotates. If the rhythm is to be increased or decreased, the change must be made gradually without jerks or sudden movements.

Remember that the spoke must turn in the hand or the rope will become so twisted and kinked that it will stop spinning. Hold the end loosely in the hand all the time and relax the grip entirely for a fraction of a second with each spin, thus enabling the spoke to revolve of its own accord. You may even turn the spoke with your fingers each time the loop makes a revolution, but this should not be necessary if you are handling the end lightly enough—the spoke should be so held as to revolve in the hand of its own accord. If the rope is guided by the thumb and forefinger there is little danger of gripping the end too tightly or using too much arm motion in spinning.

At first you will succeed in doing no more than wrapping the rope around your neck. But do not be discouraged—if you give up easily you will never be a roper. There is no easy road to roping—the ropes are stubborn and can be trained and controlled only by practice and still more practice. You may be sure that every roper has purchased his tricks by endless hours of labor— joyous labor, but labor nevertheless. So keep at it—success will come suddenly and when you least expect it. Some day when you are repeating the motions over and over, apparently hopelessly, you will let out a shout of exultation for without warning the rope suddenly begins to spin.

There are so many separate movements to watch in getting the knack of roping. We spend considerable time learning one movement, then another, and so on, without being able to do the thing as a whole. Then we suddenly succeed in integrating

these component movements and mastering the whole set in one
or two trials. So when you are most discouraged, success may
be very much closer than you think possible. Without warning
you will start spinning the rope, and from then on the trick is
yours.

Another Method of Starting the Wedding Ring.—Here is a
simple method of learning the Wedding Ring that is popular in
some places. While it is seldom used by good ropers, some teach-
ers of roping prefer to use it when giving beginners their first
initiation, feeling it is more certain of success than the regular
method, and that the standard method can be picked up easily
later on.

The question puzzling the average beginner in figuring out
the Wedding Ring is how to get inside the spinning noose. Arrange the rope on the ground in just the position that it would
be when spinning, allowing about three feet of rope for the spoke.
Then stand in the center, pick up the end of the spoke and the
loop in the right hand, and hold up the loop with the left hand.
Now turn the body suddenly to the left, raising the hands slightly
—this will lift the noose off the floor and start it floating around
the body. A turn of about forty-five degrees is all that is necessary to set the loop in motion. As you turn, release the noose
with both hands, and raise the right hand gradually up in front
of the face and behind the head, and then up to its normal position directly overhead. Don't jerk the hand up too suddenly—
jerks of all kinds are fatal in roping. Once the rope is spinning
and the hand is overhead, the process continues as described for
the standard method of starting the Wedding Ring.

Wedding Ring with the Left Hand.—When the Wedding
Ring is going nicely with the right hand, transfer the spoke to
the left hand and continue spinning. This is a good way to rest
the right arm when one is forced to spin the rope for a long
period.

The Clockwise Wedding Ring.—In the Wedding Ring as described above, the rope spins in counterclockwise fashion, this
being the standard direction in all flat spinning. To spin it clock-

wise, start it with the left hand holding the spoke, following
all the instructions given above except that the directions are
reversed. When the rope is spinning with the left hand guiding
it, the spoke may be transferred to the right hand.

THE WEDDING-RING SERIES

Now that we have the Wedding Ring well in hand and can do
it smoothly, rhythmically, and effortlessly, with both the right
hand and the left, we are ready to undertake the following tricks
which use this fundamental spin as a basis. Don't try to put
the cart before the horse by getting into these maneuvers before
you claim the Wedding Ring entirely as your own. To do so
will immediately put you in water over your head. Here, as in
every athletic sport, success depends on a thorough-going schooling in fundamentals. In a sense the following tricks are frills
which dress up and make more exciting the standard Crinoline.
If you leave no question about the smoothness of your Wedding
Ring, many of these stunts can be learned in a half hour.

The ideal length of rope for any trick is affected by the height
of the roper. In each of the following stunts, the recommended
length of rope is for an adult of average height. A shorter or
taller person than the average may require a slightly shorter or
longer rope for the best results.

HAND-SHAKING

Rope—twenty feet long with a light honda.

This trick, sometimes called the Hand-around, consists of dropping the Wedding Ring to near the floor and keeping it spinning
there by passing the spoke from hand to hand around the body.
Figure 11 shows it. The trick is one of the easiest to learn and
is quite spectacular.

Get the Wedding Ring going smoothly, and then, just as the
spoke is passing your left shoulder drop your right hand down
across the front of the body to the level of the waist in front,
thus allowing the spinning noose to drop within a few inches

of the floor. Immediately grab the spoke in the left hand and carry it around behind the back. As you do so move the right hand around behind to meet the left, and quickly grab the spoke with the right hand and carry it around in front. Here grab it in the left hand and take it around in back again. Continue this process as long as you desire to keep the trick going.

This trick will take some fast grabbing with the hands but

FIGURE 11. HAND-SHAKING

otherwise is not difficult. There is just one danger—in your eagerness to pass the spoke from hand to hand, you may break the rhythm of the spinning loop. If the loop collapses or hits you it is probably because you have jerked it as you passed the spoke around you. Try to keep time with the spinning noose, and if necessary, count to yourself to help keep the rhythm. It is imperative that the hands be kept close in to the body throughout, even brushing the hips as they are moved back and forth.

An excellent way to practice this trick is to use a stick about three feet long, passing it around you rapidly from hand to hand.

The stick should extend downward from the level of the waist and should be passed with the hands at the waist level. The hands must be kept as close to the body as possible.

You will need a smooth floor on which to learn the Hand-shaking trick. The rope is sure to touch the floor at times and a rough or irregular surface will slow up the spin or stop it, whereas the loop will slide over a polished floor and not be affected. A gym floor is ideal.

Hand-Shaking to Wedding Ring.—The Hand-shaking trick should be concluded by raising the loop into the Wedding Ring again. To accomplish this, bring the spoke around in front with the right hand as usual but instead of transferring it to the left hand, raise the right hand up across the front of the body and around behind the left shoulder and then overhead. If this is done without jerking and rushing, the loop will be lifted to the level of the waist and will continue to spin in the Wedding Ring.

Hand-Shaking Clockwise.—Hand-shaking can be done backward or in clockwise fashion by starting the Wedding Ring in the clockwise direction and then dropping the rope into the Hand-shaking trick. The clockwise Wedding Ring is described above in the detailed discussion of that trick.

HAND-SHAKING AROUND ONE LEG

Rope—twenty feet long with a light honda.

The spectacular aspect of this trick belies its simplicity. It is strong in its appeal to spectators, giving the impression of being most difficult, yet it involves nothing more in the way of rope spinning skill than Hand-shaking. Any one who can do the Hand-shaking trick easily and smoothly can learn this one in five minutes.

The stunt consists of standing on one leg, holding the other leg out to one side, and performing the Hand-shaking trick around one leg—Figure 12 shows it. While the twenty-foot rope with the light honda will do the trick, it is a little easier for most people, and a little more spectacular, if done with a twenty-five-foot rope equipped with a brass honda. This is the so-called skip rope described on page 65. With the hands held near the floor, as they must be in this trick, the light rope tends to collapse more easily than it would if it had the weight of a brass honda to keep it open.

To do this trick, get the Hand-shaking spin going smoothly and rhythmically and then quickly raise the left leg far out to one side, stoop well down, and continue to spin the rope with the hands at about the level of the knee. See Figure 12. The Hand-shaking can be done from this position just as easily as when

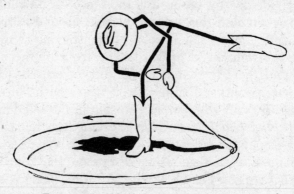

FIGURE 12.   HAND-SHAKING AROUND ONE LEG

standing upright. Pass the hands around as close to the leg as possible. Since the circumference of the leg is so much smaller than that of the body at the hips, the lowering of the spoke from the high angle to the low does not alter the length of the spoke to any material degree and consequently the sudden transition from the standing to the stooping position does not alter the size of the loop enough to break the spin.

The higher the left leg is raised the more finished and spectacular the trick appears. The leg should be held at right angles to the standing leg if possible.

Having spun the rope around the right leg a few times, lower the left leg, raise the right, and repeat the trick around the left leg.

Before attempting the trick with the rope, it is well to raise the left leg and go through the motions with the empty hand a few times.

Remember that a rough surface will be a severe handicap in learning this trick. Use a polished floor.

Variation.—Another method of Hand-shaking around One Leg consists of raising the left leg forward rather than sidewise. The body is bent slightly forward at the hips so as to enable the hands to reach low enough to pass under the raised leg. The knee of the raised leg is kept stiff. This method is neither as convenient for the performer nor as satisfying to the spectator as the first method—it seems strained, forced, and awkward.

HAND-SHAKING AROUND ALTERNATE LEGS

Rope—twenty-five feet long with a brass honda, or twenty feet long with a light honda.

Although this excellent and spectacular trick can be done well enough with the twenty-foot Wedding Ring rope it is best performed with a twenty-five-foot rope equipped with a brass honda (see the description of the skip rope on page 65). Before attempting the trick with the skip rope, it will be necessary to practice the Wedding Ring a few times with this rope, since the heavy honda will add complications for a person who is familiar only with the light-weight rope.

Get the Hand-shaking trick going nicely, then bend far down and raise the left leg forward, allowing the knee to bend, and pass the spoke around the right leg once as in Handshaking; immediately drop the left leg and raise the right, then pass the spoke around the left leg. Continue to raise the legs alternately in this way, passing the spoke once around each leg each time. Figure 13 shows the trick in action.

This trick should not be attempted until Hand-shaking around One Leg can be done easily. It will offer no serious difficulty provided the raised foot is placed as near as possible to the stationary foot each time it is put down. If a straddling motion is used, the feet being placed far apart, the hands will be forced to jerk the rope so much that the spin may be broken. This trick is a little more difficult to learn and perform than those discussed thus far in this chapter.

Be sure to practice on a smooth floor while learning.

Variation.—In performing this version of the trick described above, stand erect while doing the Hand-shaking trick, then swing the left leg up in front, keeping the knee stiff. With the left leg

FIGURE 13.   HAND-SHAKING AROUND ALTERNATE LEGS

in this position, pass the spoke around the right thigh once, using the same motion as in Hand-shaking. Immediately place the left leg down and swing the right leg up, passing the spoke around the left thigh, and so forth.

This trick is a little easier to perform than the first method described above, but it is not at all comparable in the effect it creates. It is interesting only as a little variation which one can throw into a demonstration of the Wedding-ring series of spins.

LYING DOWN

Rope—sixteen feet long with a light honda.

This trick is interesting always and involves nothing more in the way of rope spinning than the Wedding Ring. It consists of lying down with the spinning rope and taking it easy as the roper is doing in Figure 14.

While standing, start the Wedding Ring in the usual manner. When it is going nicely, drop slowly down to the knees and then to a sitting position, working the legs slowly and carefully out under the spinning noose. When everything is under control, ease the body down onto one elbow as the roper in the picture is doing. This is enough to make a good stunt out of it, but if your rope is of the right length, it will be possible for you to drop the head down to the ground and lie completely prostrate.

The difficulty presented by this stunt centers around preventing the spinning noose from touching the body. Speeding up the spinning tends to elevate the noose and lift it away from the

FIGURE 14. LYING DOWN

body. The speed should be increased gradually, however, and care taken not to break the rhythm suddenly.

Success in this stunt depends on having a rope that is just the right length for the individual who is using it. The sixteen-foot length recommended may be too short for a very tall person and too long for a short person. The rope must be long enough to make possible the Wedding Ring while standing erect. When lying down, if the spinning loop hits the body in spite of all that can be done the rope is obviously too long and must be shortened. Study what happens when you do the trick, and then experiment with the rope until just the right length is determined. Different lengths are required by different individuals.

RETIRING

Rope—sixteen feet long with a light honda.

This spectacular variation of Lying Down savors of the Wild West shows and circuses. While it can properly be done by a stunt roper, it more appropriately falls under the duties of the clown cowboy who apes the ropers' antics.

The trick consists of taking off your coat and ten-gallon hat while spinning the Wedding Ring, then lying down and using the coat as a pillow while you keep the rope spinning. Spin the Wedding Ring as usual with the right hand. With the left hand throw the coat off the left shoulder and work the left arm out of the sleeve; then transfer the rope from the right hand to the left, and slip the right arm out of the sleeve. This accomplished, sit down as described in Lying Down, roll up the coat, take off the hat, and proceed to lie down, resting your head on the coat. After spinning the rope for a moment or two in this position, sit up and put on your hat, pick up the coat, get on your feet and put on the coat again. Of course the rope must be kept spinning throughout.

THE JUGGLE

Rope—twenty feet long with a light honda.

We now come to one of the more colorful tricks of roping, much used by the expert performers. It really is not a separate spin in itself, but a flourish of the loop used in connection with the Wedding Ring. It consists of floating the Wedding Ring up and down from near the floor to over the head. Figure 15 indicates the up-and-down movement of the loop. The Juggle is beautiful and graceful indeed when skillfully done.

Using the twenty-foot rope with the light honda, get the Wedding Ring going as smoothly and rhythmically as possible. Now lower the right arm until the elbow hits the ribs in front of the right side of the body—do not turn the forearm down but keep it in a perpendicular position or nearly so. This lowering of the arm drops the loop to the level of the knees. Here give it a spin and then raise the arm up to full length, thus throwing the loop up overhead. When the loop is at the highest point give it a spin to help it along, then drop the arm again.

The rope makes four spins in the process of its up-and-down motion—one at the level of the knees, the second at the level of the waist as in the Wedding Ring, the third over the head, and the fourth at the level of the waist again. Figure 16 may serve to make this series clear. The lowering and raising of the arm

FIGURE 15. THE JUGGLE

must be done in rhythm with the spinning noose—if it is jerked or forced the loop will go lopsided or touch the body.

This is not the easiest of tricks to learn and the time required by many to get the knack of it proves disconcerting. Do not attempt to float the loop to the full extremities of the up-and-down motion at the start of the trick, but rather work into the motion gradually. In lowering the loop the tendency is to drop the right arm down to the side of the body with the hand at the level of the waist. When we recall that the right hand is held directly over the head in the Wedding Ring, it becomes

obvious that throwing the hand down and to the right side of
the body carries it far away from the center of the loop, with the
result that the loop hits the body. In lowering the arm bring
the elbow down so that it is against the ribs in front of the
right side; then turn the wrist down and lower the forearm just
enough to give the loop a spin, whereat the arm is raised to full

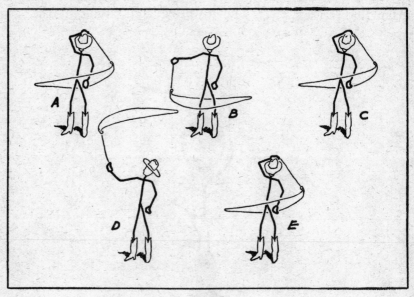

FIGURE 16. SEQUENCE OF SPINS IN THE JUGGLE

length upward with the hand directly over the head. It is well
to rise on the tiptoes as the loop is lifted.

Do not try for too much speed. Set the rhythm with the
Wedding Ring and then keep this rhythm constant. Remember
that the loop makes four spins in completing its circuit, and there
is no way to increase the speed of the up-and-down motion without increasing the rhythm of the spinning. When this trick is
properly done the loop floats gracefully and smoothly up and
down. To rush it unmakes the graceful picture.

THE BOUNCE

Rope—twenty-five feet long with a brass honda.

The Bounce is nothing more than the Juggle done more rapidly with a heavy rope. Using a twenty-five-foot rope with a brass honda, proceed just as in the case of the Juggle. The heavy honda makes possible a much greater speed. In dropping the right hand in this trick, lower it to the level of the waist and immediately swing it to the left and up behind the left shoulder. It is then carried to its full extent overhead where it gives the loop a spin and starts down again. In other words, the hand follows a corkscrew course up and down. The rope should go from the level of the knees up to the full length of the spoke overhead. There is a spring in the spoke of a spinning rope which is utilized in throwing the loop up and down.

With practice it will be possible to bounce the rope in two spins, one near the knees and the other overhead, rather than in four as in Juggling. Done rapidly and vigorously in this way, the loop zigzags up and down in most spectacular fashion.

THE HURDLE

Rope—twenty-five feet long with a brass honda, or twenty-one feet long with a medium-heavy honda.

Here is one of the finest tricks of roping—in fact, it shares. the spotlight with the Skip (Chapter III) as one of the two feature attractions in any roping exhibition. It is a strenuous, rugged stunt with much of athletic appeal—an exhilarating feat for the best of men. The cowboys in some parts call it Jumping the Spoke.

Opinions vary regarding the best rope for this trick. My own taste is for the skip rope, twenty-five feet long equipped with a brass honda (see page 65). This makes a fast and spectacular stunt of it. It can be done with a rope of about twenty-one feet, with a medium-heavy honda, and some feel that such a rope makes the trick easier to learn and to do. The medium-heavy honda is made by wrapping copper wire around the light honda on the

Wedding-Ring rope. My advice is to try the trick with the skip rope first.

The Hand-shaking trick should be mastered before this one is undertaken. Start the Wedding Ring and when the rope settles down to smooth action, drop the loop to near the floor just as was done in the Hand-shaking. The time to drop it is just as the spoke goes past the left shoulder on its way around behind

FIGURE 17. HURDLING THE SPOKE

you. At the same time that you drop your arm, bend well down and as the honda comes around, step over it with the left foot, throwing the right leg up behind. As the spoke comes around again, step over it with the right foot, and so on. Continue to jump the spoke in this way as long as you care to continue the trick. Figure 17 shows how the stunt appears.

You will have to bend down quickly at the start in order to be ready for the spoke when it comes around. The chief difficulty in this trick is getting it started—if you succeed in making the first jump, the rest will go along easily.

The spinning hand is held about a foot above the floor during

this stunt, consequently the body is bent well down and the
back foot is thrown high behind at each step. The heavy honda
makes the rope spin rapidly, thus requiring some fast stepping.
It is possible to travel across the floor and back while hurdling
the spoke, or you can run in a circle around the spinning hand
as a pivot.

At the end of the trick, stand erect and bring the loop up into
the Wedding Ring.

If a light-honda rope is used, the speed of the spin is slowed
up considerably. In this case, it is not necessary to bend down
so far, the spinning hand being held about midway between the
knees and the hips.

Be sure to practice on a polished floor.

Variation.—In this version of the Hurdle, the spoke is jumped
with both feet, rather than stepped over with one foot. The
procedure is exactly as described above except that the body is
not bent forward at the hips, but rather crouched a little at
the knees, the trunk remaining upright. The spinning hand is
held a few inches above the level of the knees. As the spoke
comes around, spring in the air with both legs, throwing the
legs high up behind and allowing the spoke to pass underneath.
As the feet come down, both strike the floor simultaneously.

This trick is much used by the stunt ropers but it is not quite
so graceful and pleasing as the standard Hurdle described in the
preceding section.

SPINNING THE BIG LOOP

*Rope—seventy to one-hundred feet of Number 10 spot cord
with a brass honda.*

Here is one of the greatest of the roping tricks in the thrill
it invariably gives the spectators. No matter how many or how
varied the tricks in a ropers' repertoire, none of them will be
more certain to "bring down the house" than the Big Loop.
And like so many roping tricks, its spectacular qualities give
the impression of its being much more difficult than it really is.
This one calls for nothing more intricate than the Wedding

Ring, although it does require muscle and endurance, and these in plentiful quantities.

The length of rope an individual will be able to spin can be determined only by experimentation, the idea in this trick being to spin the longest rope possible. Here we use Number 10 spot cord (cotton sash cord)) instead of the Number 12 size, which latter is standard in all other roping tricks. Being lighter, a longer rope can be handled in the Number 10 size. Secure one-hundred feet and try to spin it, and when you determine the amount of the rope you can let out without breaking down, cut off the

FIGURE 18. BIG LOOP

excess. It will take a rangy and very strong man to spin one-hundred feet of rope—seventy feet will offer trouble aplenty for the average person. The section trimmed off from the hundred-foot length can be used to make a light-weight skip rope (see page 65).

A rope of this length will require a very heavy honda. Secure a standard brass honda (Figure 2) from any western cowboy outfitter or spinning-rope manufacturer, and double the end of the rope around it so that there is an overlapping end of six or seven inches. Wire this end to the standing part with copper wire, wrapping the wire tightly and closely together all the way from the honda to the end. The weight of the wire and of the overlapping rope, added to that of the brass honda, will provide weight enough to dilate the big loop.

Now to spin it: Hold on to the honda and throw the rope out across the floor so that it lies straight, is free from kinks, and is unhampered by any obstructions. Form a loop about ten feet in diameter and start the rope spinning just as in the ordinary Wedding Ring. No difficulty should be encountered in starting it although much more force will be required in giving it the initial spin than is ordinarily the case. As soon as your right hand is overhead, start letting out rope *immediately*—it is necessary to move quickly here because the honda is so very heavy that it will collapse a small loop. Continue to let out rope with each spin until the entire rope is out and spinning. With the heavy honda pulling as it does, the letting out of rope is very simple, easier in fact than keeping the loop of uniform size. With each spin release the spoke momentarily and a foot or so of rope will slip out.

This is one stunt in which it is necessary to swing the right arm vigorously in a wide circle around the head until the rope is out. A decided sway of the entire body is necessary to keep the rope going. If the loop seems to get out of control as you are increasing its size, stop letting out rope and give it a few spins until it is subdued and is acting normally again.

Put this spin on with all the showmanship you have. Work hard and let the crowd know you are laboring. Even though you can do the stunt easily, it never pays to let it appear to be easy—that cheapens the trick. This principle does not hold in doing the graceful spins with a light rope; then the opposite is true, but in this heavy stunt it goes far to make the feat impressive. The mistake many professional ropers make is to perform their heavy-rope stunts with too little effort, which makes the maneuvers appear lighter and easier than they really are. The average roper will have no difficulty on this point, because he will be working plenty hard enough to show it in doing the Big Loop—and for reasons.

An elevation of some sort will make possible the spinning of a longer rope than can be accomplished on the level of the ground. A gym horse or a low stepladder will serve very well. Here a nice effort can be obtained by having a number of people stand inside the loop.

Big Loop on Horseback.—Standing on the back of a horse, it is easily possible for a strong man to let out one-hundred feet of rope, the big loop encircling the horse and spinning near the level of the ground.

The most flashy spot in a Wild West show is when a roper spins the Big Loop while standing on horseback, and then rides the horse around the arena at full gallop. This is a stunt that only the best and most athletic of ropers can do.

THE FLAT-LOOP SERIES

In the tricks described in the preceding section the roper stands inside the spinning loop. The maneuvers in this section differ in that the roper stands outside the loop and manipulates it around his body.

Prerequisite to the learning of these tricks is a thorough-going mastery of the Flat Loop by both hands (see page 23).

THE MERRY-GO-ROUND

Rope—fourteen to sixteen feet long with a light honda.

Here we have an interesting and colorful trick that every roper will want to learn. It is not only a good feature in itself but is much used as a transition from one trick to another in a rope-spinning exhibition. It consists of carrying the Flat Loop all the way around the body as illustrated in Figure 19.

While the trick can be done with the fourteen-foot rope used in learning the Flat Loop, a sixteen-foot length will be the better size for the average person, this being the length needed for the tricks in the Combination Series which follows, in which series the Merry-go-round plays an important part.

Start the Flat Loop, counterclockwise as usual, in front of the body and wait until it is going slowly, smoothly, and rhythmically. Then carry the loop around to the left and past the left side where it is given one spin. Then allow it to continue around past the back of the body and over to the right side. Here it is given another spin and is brought around in front again where the series is started over. The rope should make four spins in making the circuit of the body, one in front, one at the left side, one at the back, and one at the right side—A, B, C, and D in Figure 19 indicates this sequence of spin.

There are several things to watch in learning this trick: First off, all movements must be made smoothly and gently. There is always the fear that the rope will not get past the back of the body

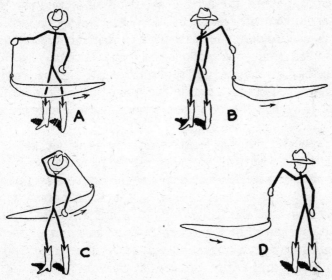

FIGURE 19. THE MERRY-GO-ROUND, SHOWING THE SEQUENCE OF SPINS

before it stops spinning, with the result that it is given a quick jerk to hurry it past, and this, of course, breaks the spin. You will probably hesitate when you get the rope to the left side of the body, holding it while you give it several turns to increase the speed of the spinning so that the loop will carry past the back. There is no more certain way to defeat the trick. The slow rhythm of the loop as it spins in front of the body must be maintained throughout. The rhythm of this spinning determines the speed at which the loop should be carried around the body; that is, the speed of the spoke as the loop revolves sets the speed for carrying the loop around the body.

As the loop reaches the left side give it one gentle spin, this spin being given as the spoke *goes back* and is on the *far* side, the side *away from the body*. With this same motion carry the spoke around in back. Don't worry about the rope getting past the back—its momentum will carry it past easily. When the loop is behind the back the arm is arched back over the head, being bent at the elbow so that the hand is as far down behind the head as it can be conveniently extended. As the hand passes behind the head it is well to turn the wrist over so that the palm is up—this helps in overcoming the tendency to jerk and rush. As the loop passes the back, the honda and spoke are on the far side, away from the body—when in this position the movement of the arm across the back in reality gives the loop a spin. Lean backward a little as the rope goes past the back.

Just after the arm has passed the right shoulder, lower your elbow down to your ribs, then extend the forearm down and out to the right and give the loop a spin at the right side. Here again the spin is given as the spoke passes on the far side, away from the body—in this case the spoke will be going forward. As soon as the loop reaches the beginning position in front of the body, start it without hesitation on another circuit around the body.

Throughout the entire process be sure to face in the same direction—don't succumb to the tendency to turn with the rope.

This trick should be practiced until it can be done easily and without conscious effort. It is a beautiful, graceful maneuver when properly done. The effort should always be for grace of movement rather than speed. Between tricks in an exhibition of flat spins, the Merry-go-round is used as a rest movement and in order to make the transition from trick to trick appear smooth and unforced. This being the case, it should be so completely mastered that it requires no attention or strained effort, and can be done with the utmost grace and ease.

With the development of skill it will be possible to carry the loop around the body in three spins instead of four.

Some may find the learning of this trick a little discouraging, but here, as in all roping, there is only one possible way to defeat discouragement and that is to practice. It is not considered a particularly difficult stunt. Study your movements carefully as you practice and try to find out just what your arm is doing. Then read these instructions over again. Soon you will be surprised to find yourself doing the trick.

Backward Merry-Go-Round.—Once the Merry-go-round is perfected as described above, it will require but very little practice to do the trick with the left hand carrying the loop around the body in the opposite direction. In this trick the rope is spun as usual in the counterclockwise direction.

It is also possible to spin the rope backward (clockwise) and carry it around the body in both directions.

TWO-HANDED MERRY-GO-ROUND

Rope—sixteen feet long with a light honda.

This is a delightful variation of the Merry-go-round, which one can claim as his own in half an hour of practice, once the basic Merry-go-round is mastered. It consists of carrying the spinning loop around the body below the level of the waist by passing the spoke from hand to hand.

Start the Flat Loop with the right hand. Transfer the spoke to the left hand, and with this hand carry the spinning loop over to the left of the body and around behind the back, keeping the hand below the level of the waist. Here take it in the right hand and bring it around in front, where the left hand takes it again and carries it around in back. After the left hand takes the rope it is necessary to give the loop one spin at the left side before carrying it around to the back.

Backward Two-Handed Merry-Go-Round.—Spin the rope in the opposite direction—clockwise—and carry it around the body in the opposite direction.

THE COMBINATION SERIES

It will be noted that the Wedding-Ring Series consists of a number of tricks in which the roper stands inside the spinning noose, whereas the Flat-Spin Series is made up of maneuvers in which the roper is outside the loop. The Combination Series consists of stunts in which the roper is inside the loop part of the time and outside part of the time. These tricks are made up of both the Wedding Ring and the Flat Loop.

JUMPING INTO THE FLAT LOOP

Rope—sixteen feet long with a light honda.

The first thought that comes into one's mind when he can do the Flat Loop is to jump into it, thus turning the Flat Loop into

FIGURE 20. JUMPING INTO THE FLAT LOOP

the Wedding Ring. And this is by no means difficult provided the jump is made at just the right moment. Unless you jump at precisely the right instant the spoke will be in the way and will hit you.

The rope in A, Figure 20, is in the right position for the step in. Note that the spoke is on the *far* side, away from the roper, and is just starting toward him. If you step when the honda is in this position, it will have passed you and be out of the way by the time you actually enter the loop.

It is a case of *stepping into the loop*, not of jumping up and pulling the rope under you, which latter movement would throw the loop lopsided. Spring lightly over into the loop as the roper is doing in B, Figure 20, the rope remaining in the same place throughout. Once you are in it, raise the right hand overhead and do the Wedding Ring.

With practice you will be able to tell when the jump should be made by the feel of the rope in your hand, thus making it unnecessary to watch it.

A polished floor will be a decided help in learning this trick.

JUMPING OUT

Rope—sixteen feet long with a light honda.

After you have jumped into the Flat Loop and are thus spinning the Wedding Ring, the next move is to jump out again. To accomplish this, drop the loop down to the floor and then step backward and out of it, continuing to spin the rope in the Flat Loop in front. The time to lower the rope is just as it passes your left shoulder. As you step back and out, lean well forward so as to be in position to do the Flat Spin.

Remember that it is a case of stepping out of the loop, not of jumping up and pulling the loop forward from under you. The loop is spinning in the same position after you are out as it was before.

When you have learned to jump in and jump out, you can go in and out in rapid succession. As soon as you are in, give the Wedding Ring one spin and then step out, whereat the Flat Loop is given one spin and you step in again.

An interesting variation here is to do the Hand-shaking trick instead of the Wedding Ring after stepping in. When the spoke comes around as you step in, take it in your left hand and carry it around as in Hand-shaking. As soon as your right hand takes the spoke, step out again. In this maneuver the loop is not raised more than a foot from the floor throughout.

TAPPING IN AND OUT

Rope—sixteen feet long with a light honda.

This maneuver involves nothing more in the way of roping than the ordinary Flat Loop but it is an interesting and spectacular maneuver. It consists of stepping into the Flat Loop with one foot and immediately withdrawing it to let the spoke pass. This trick should be easy enough once it is possible to spin the Flat Loop and jump into it. It should not be attempted before jumping into the Flat Loop is learned.

Spin the Flat Loop in front of the body. Lean well forward and raise the right foot in readiness to step forward. The time to step is the same as in Jumping into the Flat Loop—just as the spoke reaches the far side and starts toward you; it will be past and out of the way by the time you have stepped. Keep your eye on the spoke constantly and get its rhythm. At the proper second, shove the right foot in and tap the floor, immediately withdrawing it to let the spoke pass. As soon as the spoke passes, insert it again, tapping the floor with it as before. Practice until you can tap it in the loop regularly without a miss or without losing the rhythm.

When you can tap the right toe in the loop in this manner, try stepping in and taking the weight on the right foot, then immediately withdrawing it. Do not lift the left foot from the floor at first, but merely throw the weight on the right foot. Later, do the finished trick by stepping in with the right foot and at the same time throwing the left foot high up behind. Then step back on the left foot and raise the right to let the spoke pass. This is a spectacular stunt when done rapidly. It is extremely effective if time is kept to music.

We now come to the third method of doing this trick, and it is by all odds the most colorful one, not to say the most difficult. Step in with the right foot, placing the weight on it but keeping the left foot on the floor. As the spoke comes around, jump in the air with both feet, reverse the position of the feet, and land on both feet with the left foot in the loop. The spoke passes while you are in the air. As soon as you land, leap up again, reverse the position of the feet and land with the right foot in the loop.

This trick will furnish lots of interest and plenty of exercise. It is within the capacity of every athletic person and can be learned early in one's roping experience, in that it calls for nothing more in the way of roping skill than the Flat Loop and Jumping In. Be sure to practice it on a polished floor.

UP AND OVER

Rope—sixteen feet long with a light honda.

We now come to one of those tricks that give character and spectacle to the flat spins. It consists of jumping into the Flat

FIGURE 21. UP AND OVER

Loop and immediately throwing the loop up over the head, then down in front to the Flat Loop again. Figure 21 shows it.

Spin the Flat Loop a little faster than is normally the case and get it going smoothly with the loop directly parallel with the floor. Give it a good spin as you step into it and immediately throw the arm up over the head—this throws the loop high up in the air as in B, Figure 21. Give it a spin while it is at its highest point, then throw it sharply down to the floor in front and pick up the Flat Loop again as in C, Figure 21. Figure 21 is misleading to the extent that the roper does not turn around in throwing the rope to the floor as C would indicate, but rather faces in the same direction throughout and throws the loop down to the same position it was in before the jump was made.

As in every complicated trick, there are several items to watch in this maneuver: Be sure the Flat Loop is spinning briskly before you step into it—if it is moving slowly and lazily it will not have momentum enough to keep going as it is thrown up. The last spin before you step must give it the force to carry it, but be sure that this last spin is a *circular* spin—there is always danger that you will pull it toward you and upward instead of spinning it perfectly. When you step into it, raise your back foot high and pull it in quickly or it will catch the rope. Further, keep your hand and arm close in to your body as you throw the rope up. The hand normally goes diagonally across from the right hip to the left shoulder, then up past the left side of the head to a point directly overhead, following a sort of corkscrew course as it goes up.

When the rope is overhead, look up at it and give it one spin there as the roper is doing in B, Figure 21, then immediately throw it down in front. Be sure to practice on a polished floor. While learning, throw the loop down directly onto the floor, then jerk it up immediately into the Flat Spin. As skill is acquired, you will be able to stop the loop in the air by starting the Flat-loop motion with the arm as the loop comes down.

JUGGLING UP AND OVER

Rope—sixteen feet long with a light honda.

This trick starts from the Wedding Ring and terminates by the rope being thrown up overhead, then down in front to the Flat Spin. It is a variation of the Up and Over.

Start the Wedding Ring and go into the Juggle (page 41), taking plenty of time to get the loop under control. When the loop is at the lowest point, give it a good spin and throw the arm up over head just as in the Up and Over. Aside from the start of the trick, it is in no respect different from the standard

Up and Over.   The details of the Up and Over are discussed in the preceding section.

LIFT ONTO BODY

Rope—twenty feet long with a light honda.

The two Up-and-Over tricks just described are in reality "lifts" in that the noose is carried upward, but they differ from the present one in that in those tricks the roper is inside the loop, whereas in this one, the loop is spun in front and is thrown up and then down around the body.   This is a difficult trick to learn, so much so that it is well to delay it until after the Skip described in the next chapter is learned.

We must now give attention for the first time to a principle of roping concerning which we shall have much to say in the chapter on the vertical spins, and one which must be understood before success in this trick will be possible.

If you were to spin the Flat Loop in front of you and then suddenly throw the loop a few feet straight upward, it is obvious that the loop would hit your spinning arm and as a result fall to the floor collapsed.   But if, as you raise the loop, you would carry the right hand and the spoke to one side, the loop could pass upward unhampered.   You could then reach inside the spinning loop from underneath and continue the spinning from within. Here you have the idea of this trick and also an understanding of a movement necessary in many of the vertical spins.   As a matter of fact, the two Up-and-Over tricks just described involve this principle—when the loop is thrown from its highest point down to the floor there is a possibility that the loop will hit the spoke. However, the downward throw tends to pull the spoke over to one side without the roper's paying any attention to the process, and consequently there is no need of discussing the matter in that connection.

A twenty-foot rope should be used with an end of three feet extending over into the left hand, thus making the length of the spinning section about seventeen feet.   Start the Flat Loop in the usual way and turn so that the loop is to the right side of the body. Take plenty of time to get the spin going in perfect rhythm and try to absorb the feeling of its rhythm yourself. Lean forward, keeping your eye on the position of the honda. Just as the honda starts forward (toward the direction you are facing) raise the right hand smartly, *first upward and then toward the left,* so that it comes to rest directly in front of the forehead and an inch or two above the level of the head, the arm extending well out to the front. This movement of the hand will carry the spoke

FIGURE 22. LIFT ONTO BODY

outside the loop and at the same time will throw the loop up above the right hand. Now, by bending the elbow, pull the right hand sharply toward the forehead until it almost touches it, and at the same time give the loop a spin with the wrist. The result will be to pull the loop down over the head into the usual Wedding Ring around the body. Figure 22 may help you to understand the movements.

No, this trick will not be performed the first time it is tried— that would be nothing but an accident. It will take repeated practice coupled with constant study of the reasons for failures.

Do not spin the Flat Loop too rapidly at the start of the trick.

When the moment arrives to lift it upward, however, do not hesitate—it must be thrown up smartly and definitely. From the time the loop is lifted until it falls over the head, it makes only one revolution, and consequently there is no time to be wasted. The lift is not a question of sudden, forceful jerks—in fact, but very little muscle is used—but rather of perfect timing and decisive action. There is a spring in the spoke of a spinning noose that is utilized here to send the loop upward sharply, and then to pull it down over the head with equal definiteness. The whole movement, however, must be done in the same rhythm as set by the Flat Loop at the start—try to get the feel of the rhythm from the spoke as it moves around and to swing the hand upward with about the same rate of speed with which the honda revolves. Once you are sure your movements are correct in detail, experiment with the speed of the lift, for it is this question of timing that will require the most practice.

Keep at this trick. It can't be purchased cheaply.

LIFT ONTO ARM

Rope—sixteen feet long with a light honda.

In this trick the Flat Loop is lifted and then dropped around the right arm and spun there, rather than around the body—Figure 23 shows it clearly. What really happens is that after the loop is lifted, the Wedding Ring is spun around the right arm instead of around the entire body. Do not attempt this trick until the Lift onto Body has been learned.

Using a sixteen-foot rope, start a small Flat Loop in front of the body, not over two-and-one-half feet in diameter, allowing the excess rope to extend over into the left hand—see A, Figure 23. Raise the loop directly upward, timing the lift exactly as in the Lift onto Body. As the loop comes up, move the hand a little to the left, thus drawing the spoke out so that the loop does not hit it. Then shove the hand abruptly under the loop and into the center of it—the loop will drop around the arm and a tiny Wedding Ring will be spinning. Figure 23 shows the general movement.

To throw the little Wedding Ring into a Flat Loop again, drop the right arm suddenly and withdraw the spoke. When the loop has fallen, pick up the flat spin in front of the body as usual.

FIGURE 23. LIFT ONTO ARM

THE SKYROCKET

Rope—sixteen feet long with a light honda.

This is a spectacular and none-too-easy flourish of the rope in which the Flat Loop is lifted and carried over the top of the head and down to the opposite side of the body. It differs from the Lift onto Body in that the loop, once lifted, is not dropped over the body into the Wedding Ring but, rather, is carried across the top of the head and then dropped into the Flat Loop again. It is a good trick to learn after the Lift onto Body has been mastered, but will be confusing indeed if attempted before.

Using a sixteen-foot rope, spin the Flat Loop in front of the body, counterclockwise as usual. Carry it over to the left side of the body and let it settle down into a steady rhythm there. Just as the spoke is passing backward (that is, when it is on the side of the loop away from the body) raise the right hand directly upward with a decisive movement. By the time the lift can be made the spoke will be on the near side of the loop and moving forward. Raise the right hand first straight upward, then a little to the right so as to draw the spoke out of the way of the loop. This throws the loop up over the level of the head to the left of the body. With this same movement of the hand to the right, shove the right arm across over the top of the head—this will carry the loop across also. Immediately drop the right hand down to the level of the waist, thus pulling the loop down to the right side of the body into the usual Flat Loop.

As in all the Lifts, the arm must be raised sharply and definitely, yet without jerks. There can be no hesitation from the start of the trick to the finish. The swinging of the right hand up across the head and down is done with one continuous sweep. The rhythm of the spoke in the Flat Loop sets the speed of the hand as it lifts the loop—this same speed is continued as the hand moves up, over the head, and down. The loop makes one spin as it crosses the head, and one as it falls.

A little difficulty may be encountered in preventing the loop from hitting the spoke as it falls to the right, but by studying the position of the spoke as one practices, the proper movement can be easily figured out. By the time one has mastered the art of withdrawing the spoke in the Lift onto Body, he will understand the principle well enough to apply it in this trick.

As soon as the rope has dropped to the right side in the Flat Loop, carry it around to the left side again and start the trick over.

English literature on roping refers to this stunt under the title of Sun-fishing.

CHAPTER III

Rope Spinning—The Vertical Spins

This chapter opens up the second stage in a roper's learning experience, the first stage being confined to flat spins described in the last chapter. In the vertical spins, the rope is spun so that the loop is perpendicular to the floor.

So spectacular are these vertical spins that every beginner is eager to master them as early in his roping experience as possible, and rightly so, for here is roping at its best. More than anything else the vertical spins label one as a master of the art of roping and entitle him to the classification of being out of the amateur stage.

Yet it will be obvious to all who know the first rudiments of handling a rope that these vertical maneuvers are much more difficult than most of the flat spins and consequently cannot be taken up too soon. True, some of the intricate flat spins, such as the Lifts, may prove to be more confusing than any vertical, yet the fact remains that a rather thorough schooling in flat spinning is essential before the tricks in this chapter can be undertaken with any degree of satisfaction. It would be a mistake to jump to the conclusion that these tricks are so forbidding that none but a professional can hope to learn them, for that is far beyond the fact. Once one can do a number of the flat spins these vertical stunts may offer no more of a problem than was encountered in learning the simplest of the flat tricks. Yet if they are attempted before the flat spins, they will be difficult indeed. The result would doubtless be permanent discouragement.

At the beginning of the preceding chapter, a graded list of flat spins was presented, suggesting the order in which the tricks should be learned. It need not be assumed that all of these flat spins must be learned before the various stunts in this chapter

are undertaken. After one has learned six or eight of the flat spins
he may be familiar enough with the problems offered by the lariat
to be able to pick up rather easily the famous Skip, which is not
only the feature stunt of vertical spins but the most spectacular
of all roping tricks.

GRADED LIST OF VERTICAL SPINS

Assuming that most of the flat spins described in the preceding
chapter are well in hand, the vertical tricks presented in this
chapter should be taken up in approximately the following order:

1. The Skip
2. Vertical Raise onto Body
3. The Butterfly
4. Forward-and-Backward Butterfly
5. The Arrowhead
6. Rolling Butterfly
7. The Zigzag
8. Vertical Raise onto Arm
9. The Ocean Wave
10. The Running Skip
11. Skip and Turn
12. The Rolls

THE SKIP

Rope—twenty-five feet long with a brass honda.

The Skip is the greatest trick in roping, barring none. Thrill-
ing and spectacular to the onlookers, it is the perfect finale to a
roping act. Vigorous and robust, it the best of exercise for the
performer. It consists of spinning a large loop and jumping
through it as the roper is doing in Figure 24.

I like the Skip—I like to watch it done and I like to do it. It
seems to symbolize for me the art of roping. The flying loop as
it zigzags back and forth, encircling the jumping roper, is beautiful and invigorating to behold. This is a rugged, lusty stunt—
you may be sure that the person who does it is not only a roper
but an athlete. It is one of those heavy tricks in which the movements are full, vigorous, and hard. There is none of the delicate
and precise wrist motion that is so exasperating in many of the
light tricks. Right here is one of chief reasons for its popularity
—the heavy, vigorous stunts are always more satisfying to perform
than the delicate ones and certainly they carry a greater appeal to
the onlookers. For example, the Skip is an easier trick to learn

than the delicate Butterfly, yet it is so much more spectacular and appears to be so much more difficult that it completely over-shadows the Butterfly in any roping exhibition. From the stand-point of showmanship there is no comparison between the light and heavy maneuvers—those artists who confine themselves to the delicate tricks are better ropers than they are showmen.

No, the Skip is not too difficult for one with average athletic

FIGURE 24. THE SKIP—GREATEST OF ALL ROPING TRICKS

ability. But it will take work to perfect it. That is why it is so highly valued among ropers—since it cannot be purchased cheaply, few possess it. Yet it probably is the easiest of the major tricks in this chapter, easier certainly than the Butterfly and the Rolls. In comparison to these, the vigorous, muscular characteristics of the Skip belie the ease with which it is learned. It requires just one thing—*practice*. But however much in the way of time it may cost you, it is worth it.

The Skip is really four tricks in one, and each of these stages must be learned separately: (1) the vertical spin, counterclock-wise; (2) the jump through; (3) the backward or clockwise spin;

(4) the jump back. Before we take up each of these stages in turn, however, we must discuss the making of the skip rope.

The Skip Rope.—The Skip calls for a twenty-five-foot rope with a brass honda. Ropers refer to this as the skip rope. Use Number 12 braided cotton sash cord (spot lariat cord). Occasionally an expert uses the smaller Number 10 size for the Skip, but this rope is too fast for a beginner. The Number 12 size spins more slowly and deliberately, giving the roper more time to gauge the time to jump. Secure the brass honda from any cowboy outfitter or spinning rope manufacturer. These hondas are not to be confused with the light metal eyes sold for use on ropes by hardware stores, which latter are useless for our purpose. Send for a standard brass honda made for the purpose—it should weigh at least an ounce and a half. Double the end of the rope around the honda and wire with six or seven wrappings of medium-heavy copper wire, as shown in Figure 25 and described on page 11.

FIGURE 25. BRASS HONDA FOR THE SKIP ROPE

After experimenting with the rope, if you find it so long that the spinning loop is too large for your height, either cut it down to the proper length for you, or let the end extend over into the left hand. Cut off a few inches only and try out the rope again—a few inches make a considerable difference in the size of the loop.

The Vertical Spin, Counterclockwise.—Arrange the rope as in A, Figure 26. Note that the right hand holds the loop up and that the end extends over into the left hand, thus making a rather small loop. The spoke extends about half way from the right hand down to the ground.

Give the loop a hard spin by throwing the right hand forward and downward in a semicircular course, and as you do so, release the loop with both hands, retaining hold of the spoke only. Keep the loop spinning by whirling the right hand briskly in a circle about a foot in diameter. Just the second you see that the rope is actually spinning, start letting out rope with each spin until it is all out and spinning as in B, Figure 26. It is imperative that you let out rope quickly because the honda is so heavy that it will collapse the small loop, whereas when the rope is all out the weight

FIGURE 26. STARTING THE VERTICAL SPIN

of the honda will keep the loop open and spinning steadily in the vertical position.

Weighted as the honda is, the initial spin must be much harder and more decisive than is the case in any of the light-rope tricks. In fact, more force must be used throughout the entire trick because of the greater weight of the rope, but once the rope is all out, the spinning is done entirely with the wrist, not the arm.

Beware of wild and violent arm motion. Each time the spoke comes around, give it an emphatic spin with the wrist. In a heavy vertical spin like this, one of the chief concerns is to keep the loop from dropping low enough to touch the floor. Consequently the spin is given each time that the spoke comes *up*—this tends to lift the loop up at the same time that it revolves it.

The heavy honda keeps the rope spinning in this position much more easily than one might expect. Once going, the honda does much to carry the spin. One of the reasons why a heavy trick like this is easier to do is that slight jerks which would destroy a delicate spin have no disastrous effects—the weight of the honda is great enough to overcome these irregular movements and the loop goes right on spinning.

The skip rope can be spun with great speed, and the beginner usually delights in whirling it as rapidly as possible. Here, as in all roping, however, we must practice the spin slowly, evenly, and rhythmically

Care must be exercised to keep the loop spinning in a perpendicular plane. There is often a tendency for the loop to settle down over one's head and gradually fall into the Wedding Ring. Keep the spinning arm extended almost at full length, and be sure that the wrist throws the spoke straight upward with each spin.

Do not rush into jumping through the loop. Take plenty of time to perfect the spinning before trying the jumping. You will get there more quickly if you do.

Jumping Through.—Spin the rope as described above and turn your left side toward it, reaching your right arm across in front of your body, as the roper is doing in B, Figure 26. Slow down the spinning as much as possible. Now it is a case of perfect timing: unless you jump at just the right time the spoke will hit you. The time to jump is when the spoke is going *down*. The spoke is in just the right position for the jump in A, Figure 27. By the time you have jumped, it will be going up as in B, Figure 27, and thus will be out of the way. If you wait until the spoke is going up before jumping, you will be unable to get through before it will be going down and thus be in the direct line of your jump.

As the spoke starts down, jump in the air and pull the spoke sharply toward you, thereby carrying the loop around your body and over to the other side, as shown in B, Figure 27. After you have jumped, the loop will be spinning on your other side, as in A, Figure 28.

It is not a case of jumping over into the loop, but rather of jumping straight up and pulling the loop past you. There is a spring in the spoke of a spinning loop that sends the loop flying past you when you pull it.

Here are the items to watch in learning this trick: As you pull

FIGURE 27. JUMPING THROUGH—FIRST MOVEMENT IN THE SKIP

the loop toward you, keep your hand close in to your body. Your hand goes right across the pit of your stomach and must be so close that it almost brushes it. Be sure to give the loop a hard spin on its last revolution before you jump, and then forget about the spinning. In pulling the rope to you, your hand goes straight across, or, if anything, rises a little. Beginners usually throw the loop down toward the floor for fear that it will hit the feet if they do not. There is never any danger here—the problem is to keep it up high enough so that it will not hit the floor. Jump off the floor at the same second that you pull and raise your feet high. If you give the rope an emphatic pull, draw your hand straight across and keep it close in to your stomach, and at the same time pick your feet up high, the rope cannot fail to sail past without hitting.

Don't worry about spinning the rope on the other side once you have jumped through. That is another trick and can come later. Keep practicing the spin and the jump. Practice each movement separately, and before you know it, you will be putting them all together in the completed trick.

True, the honda is heavy and moves swiftly, and if it should hit you squarely it might hurt a little. Knowing that the heavy honda is there, it takes a little courage to jump into the loop. But that is part of the game and you can be sure that the honda cannot do any severe damage.

With practice you can tell by the feel of the rope in your hand when the time arrives to jump. Then you will be doing the trick automatically and with no conscious attention.

Be sure to practice on a polished floor.

When you can spin the rope as described you have learned one half of the Skip. The next task is to learn the clockwise spin and jump back.

The Second or Clockwise Spin.—After you have jumped through the loop, the rope is spinning in the opposite direction, in respect to your position, from what it was before you jumped. It is actually spinning in the same direction, but it is going in the opposite direction *in relation to the roper*, and that is the factor that counts. Before you jumped the loop was being spun counterclockwise and after the jump, clockwise.

Since there is no need to know how to do the second or clockwise spin until you can jump through the loop, the easiest way to learn it is to jump through and then try to keep the spin going on the other side. This should offer very little difficulty because the rope is already spinning. If you were careful not to let the loop hit the floor too hard when you jumped, it should still be revolving vigorously and the only worry will be to pick up the spinning motion with your arm before the loop has slowed down too much. Having jumped, the rope is spinning on your right side. As soon as you gain your footing, look toward the rope and gain control of it as quickly as possible. Remember the emphasis in the spinning should be on the *upward* stroke; otherwise the loop will sink down and hit the floor.

No detailed instructions are necessary here. The loop is already spinning and a little practice will discover the means of keeping it going.

Jumping Back.—As with the first jump, the time to jump is when the spoke is going down. However, in this case it seems easier for most beginners to put the emphasis on the upward

FIGURE 28. JUMPING BACK—SECOND MOVEMENT IN THE SKIP

motion. As the spoke starts upward—when it is in the position shown in A, Figure 28—give it an emphatic spin and then wait a second until it has time to start downward. At this point jump in the air and give the spoke a sharp pull toward you. It will pass around you as in B, Figure 28.

The same points must be remembered here as in the first jump: Keep your right hand close in to your body, bringing it past the pit of your stomach, and pull it straight across or a little upward to prevent the loop from striking the floor. Be sure to pick your feet up high.

The Finished Skip.—Now that we have learned all the elements, we are ready to do the complete Skip. Keep the body facing in the same direction throughout, turning only the head and shoulders toward the rope. At first, spin the rope three times on each side, that is, pull the loop across in the third spin. This makes a reasonably fast trick, yet gives you time to get your bearings after each jump. As soon as you are able, do the trick by spinning the loop twice on each side, jumping on the second spin. This is the standard rhythm for the trick. In case the loop gets out of control at any point, stop jumping and spin it until it settles down again.

The Skip relies on the spring in the spinning loop for aid in pulling it back and forth. After the jump the loop flies as far to the side as the length of the spoke will permit, and here it seems to spring back of its own accord. When done in the proper rhythm of two spins on each side, the spring back starts it on its way across again, and consequently less force is needed than otherwise would be the case.

Alternative Method for the Skip.—The Skip can be done by spinning the rope in the opposite direction from that described above. That is, when the loop is on the left side, spin it clockwise, and when on the right side, counterclockwise. The general procedure is the same for both methods and any one can learn this method from the points presented above in the detailed discussion of the first method.

SKIP AND TURN

Rope—twenty-five feet long with a brass honda.

Here is the most brilliant version of the Skip. It should not replace the standard Skip but rather be used as a finishing flourish, and as such, it constitutes a dazzling finale.

Start the rope spinning in the usual way preliminary to skipping, and face the loop squarely with the body instead of turning the left side to it as in the standard Skip. Jump and pull the loop past you as in the Skip but as you do, turn in the air, doing a right-about-face so that when you land on the floor you are facing the opposite direction and are still facing the loop squarely as it spins on the other side. Now jump back as in the last half of the Skip, but turn to the right in the air again so that you are once more facing the loop as it spins on the original side. This gives a surprisingly effective flourish to the stunt.

But there is still more color to be added: Keep your feet together as you jump and land on your toes, springing right back up in the air again. Jump through the loop on every second spin, that is, spin it once and jump through on the next spin. After the jump, spring up in the air from your toes for a height of three or four inches, this spring being in time with the spin of the loop in front of you. As soon as you land from this spring, jump high and pull the loop past you. You are thus springing up in the air with every spin of the loop, skipping it on every other spin, and turning an about-face in the air as you skip. That is action enough to add spectacle to any stunt.

If this sets too fast a pace for you, jump the rope on every third spin. Certainly you will need to do that in learning.

Note that all turns in the air are made to the right. Thus when you have completed the two jumps of the full Skip, you have turned in a complete circle. The tendency is to do a left-about-face in making the second jump, but this is wrong. The first jump will offer no difficulty because, in turning to the right, the left side of the body is turned toward the loop and thus is in exactly the same position as in the standard Skip. The jump back, however, offers its problems because, in turning to the right, the left side of the body is presented to the loop whereas in the standard Skip the right side is toward it. Learn this second jump by practicing it with the standard Skip, minus the turning in the air—after you have made the first jump of the Skip, turn the *left* side toward the rope and try to jump back. Be sure to keep your rope hand close in to your body as you jump, pulling it right past the pit of your stomach.

RUNNING SKIP

Rope—twenty-five feet long with a brass honda.

Down the arena of the circus tent comes the colorful cowboy, running at top speed, the flying loop of his lariat zigzagging back and forth as he skips through it, without missing a step or slowing up in the slightest. It is the Running Skip—a headliner in any circus, and a challenge to the toughest and most strenuous of athletes.

This trick is a hard nut to crack, not that it calls for the learning of another difficult roping trick, but that it demands perfect co-ordination and a sturdy constitution.

It goes without saying that the chief prerequisite is a perfect Skip. Given this, there is nothing to stop one from trying to run with it.

Two steps are taken between skips, that is, the roper takes two running steps, makes the first jump through the loop, and so on. In other words the rope is skipped on every third step. The running must be done in rhythm with the spinning loop. Spin the loop twice and jump through on the third spin. The stepping thus coincides with the spinning, the roper taking one step for each spin and in rhythm with the spin. To be spectacular the running must be fast, and since the feet must keep time with the spinning the steps are typically long and gliding. The third step, on which the jump through takes place, is more of a jump into the air than a step, the roper bringing both feet up high beneath him.

Practice by walking rather than running. By taking short steps and not attempting to cover much ground, the movements can be practiced with fewer breakdowns. Once the movements become habitual the pressure can be applied and the run speeded up.

Perhaps the hardest movement in this trick is spinning the loop on the left side while running. It takes considerable muscular effort to spin the loop while reaching across the body with the right arm at the same time that one is running.

If you ever valued a smooth floor for roping practice, you will appreciate one here. And once you try to do this trick on a polished floor, you will appreciate what the circus cowboy is up against when he must do it over the rough and sometimes muddy ground in a circus tent.

This trick may be done by using either of the methods of doing the Skip described above. The Alternative Method for the Skip (page 71) is perhaps a little more desirable for the Running

Skip than the standard method for the reason that in this method the rope is being spun forward, in the direction of the running, and consequently the motion given the loop in spinning it tends to carry it forward.

Backward Running Skip.—This novelty is exactly like the Running Skip except that the roper moves backward. Needless to say the steps are short and the speed of movement much slower.

VERTICAL RAISE ONTO BODY

Rope—twenty-five feet with a brass honda.

Figure 29 tells the story of this movement rather clearly. It is scarcely classified as a roping trick, but it is a handy movement

FIGURE 29.   VERTICAL RAISE ONTO BODY

to know when giving a roping exhibition, in that it is often used as a transition from one trick to another.

Use the twenty-five-foot rope with its brass honda, but allow the end to extend over into the left hand, thus shortening the rope three or four feet. Start a flat loop in front of the body or one that is a cross between a flat and vertical spin, as shown in A, Figure 29. Raise the loop into a vertical spin as in B, and then continue to raise the arm until the loop is spinning over the head in a plane parallel to the floor, as in C. When in this position it will settle down into the Wedding Ring around the body of its own accord.

When the rope is spinning in the vertical plane, remember that the emphasis must be placed on the upward stroke of the arm, rather than on the downward. This not only spins the loop successfully, but tends to prevent it from sagging down toward the floor—it serves to lift the loop. The loop must be raised gradually and the lifting done in this upward stroke of the spoke.

This is, really, a very simple maneuver. In fact, it is often easier for a beginner to let a vertical spin settle down over his head into the Wedding Ring than it is to keep it spinning vertically. For example, in learning the Skip the beginner must take precautions to keep the loop spinning vertically and to prevent it from settling down over the head. That is why the Skip should be learned before the Raise—the Skip forces one to master a clean, vertical spin, which will be easier to accomplish if one has not practiced letting it drop back into a flat spin.

Just how high overhead the loop can be raised depends upon the length of the rope used. If the full length of the Skip rope is let out, it will be difficult to raise it completely over the head; what will happen is that the top of the vertical loop will settle back over the head and down behind, thus forming the Wedding Ring, without the loop flattening out into a flat spin over the top of the head. With a shorter rope, it will be possible to raise the loop higher.

VERTICAL RAISE ONTO ARM

Rope—fourteen feet long with a light metal honda.

Use a fourteen-foot rope equipped with a brass honda weighing three-fourths of an ounce or an ounce—about half the weight of the standard brass honda. This honda is made by grinding down the edges of a standard brass honda.

Spin this rope in a vertical plane, counterclockwise as usual. Raise the arm gradually until the loop is spinning around the spinning arm in a flat spin. The result is a tiny Wedding Ring around the right arm.

RAISE OFF THE BODY OR ARM

When the Raise onto Body has been completed and the loop is spinning around the body in the Wedding Ring, it can be raised off the body by gradually bringing the spinning arm back to its original position. The loop will then be spinning vertically in front of the body.

The Raise Off the Arm is done in the same way.

THE BUTTERFLY

Rope—fourteen feet long with a light honda.

The Butterfly is one of the most beautiful of the lariat tricks. Many regard it as the acme of roping grace. It is a delicate little

FIGURE 30. THE BUTTERFLY

trick, however, and consequently is considered rather difficult by most learners. Small, delicate motions requiring careful balance and timing are always more difficult to perfect than the full, strong movements. Further, the Butterfly does not stand out in a roping exhibition nearly as vividly as the larger loops, and does not give the impression of being as hard as it really is.

In the Butterfly, a small loop is spun vertically in front and to the left of the body, and then is carried across to the right side in front, then back to the left side again, and so on without interruption. The loop thus floats back and forth in a sort of figure-of-eight motion. Figure 30 may help to make it clear. The principle is the same as in the Skip except that the trick is done in front of the body without the jump through.

Use a fourteen-foot rope while learning, holding it with the end in the right hand. Start a vertical loop *clockwise* in front of the left shoulder, using a spoke about one foot long. The loop is spun at right angles to the chest, not parallel to it—study Figure 30. Start the spin at shoulder height and then allow it to drop down to the line of the waist. Try to revolve the loop as slowly as possible.

Here again the question of timing comes up. Just as the honda reaches the bottom of its revolution draw the hand across to the right and a little upward. This will carry the loop across to the right side. Unless the pull across is made just at the right moment, the spoke will be in the way and will hit the loop. If made as directed the spoke will be pulled out of the way.

When the loop reaches the right side, it will be spinning in a counterclockwise direction and the hand must pick up this spin immediately. Again, just as the honda reaches the bottom of its revolution, draw the right hand across to the left and a little upward, thus throwing the loop back to its original position. Continue to carry the loop back and forth in this way. The rule to remember is to make the reverse *when the honda is at the bottom of the loop.*

Although it may be necessary to spin the loop several times on each side while learning, the Butterfly calls for two spins on each side and this rhythm should be picked up just as early in the practice as possible. As a matter of fact, the loop makes one-and-a-half circles on each side and is carried over to the other side on the last half circle. The emphasis in spinning should always be put on the first spin on each side.

This trick is done almost entirely with the wrist. The wrist must be kept very flexible and must flow smoothly back and forth with the rhythm of the loop, without jerks or sudden movements.

Here rests the chief problem in learning the Butterfly. When a small, light loop is being spun vertically, any slight jerk will destroy it. It will take time to train the wrist so that the proper movements will be made evenly and automatically. The right hand follows a figure-of-eight course as it goes back and forth, circling twice with each loop of the eight. The body turns slightly to the left when the loop is on that side, then to the right, with a gentle, swaying motion.

It will be a great help to count as you spin the loop, saying "*One* and, two and, *one* and, two and." The loop is carried over on the second *and*. Emphasizing the *one* helps you to give greater emphasis to the first spin on each side.

The loop spins *clockwise* on the left side, and counterclockwise on the right side. In reality, it is spinning in the same direction throughout, but *in relation to your position* it spins in opposite directions on each side. There is no interruption in the spinning nor any reversal of direction—the loop merely appears to be going in opposite directions as viewed by the roper.

It may help to visualize the proper time to carry the loop across if you think of the spinning loop as the face of a clock. The time to carry the hand across is when the honda reaches *six o'clock*. This applies to both sides.

THE BUTTERFLY—FORWARD AND BACKWARD

Rope—fourteen feet long with a light honda.

In the standard Butterfly the loop is carried back and forth from left to right in front of the body. It can also be done forward and backward.

Start a vertical spin clockwise in front of the right shoulder so that the plane of the loop is parallel to the plane of the chest. The movement is exactly as in the standard Butterfly except that the loop is pulled back past the right side, from which point it is carried forward again. The timing is exactly as in the Butterfly, the loop being reversed when the honda is at the bottom of its revolution, that is, when it is in the six o'clock position.

The same trick can be done at the left side of the body, which latter should be as thoroughly mastered as the right-side motion in that it leads up to and serves as a foundation for the picturesque Arrowhead, the next trick to be learned. Spin the loop clockwise in front of the left shoulder and carry it backward past the left side, then forward again.

Both of these tricks can be learned very quickly once the standard Butterfly is well in hand. They will then involve nothing new in the way of roping.

FIGURE 31. THE ARROWHEAD

THE ARROWHEAD

Rope—fourteen feet long with a light honda.

This is a combination of the standard Butterfly and the Forward-and-Backward Butterfly.

Start the trick as in the Forward-and-Backward Butterfly: spin the loop clockwise in front of the right shoulder and carry it backward past the right side. When it is brought forward again, it is drawn to front and center of the body, and from here it is carried back past the left side. The rope follows the course shown in Figure 31. This course forms an arrowhead, hence the name of the trick. It is sometimes referred to as the Triangular Butterfly.

Any one who can do a good Butterfly will have no trouble in learning this trick.

REVERSING THE BUTTERFLY

Rope—fourteen feet long with a light honda.

The best way to reverse the direction of the loop in the Butterfly is to reverse the direction of the *body*. Spin the standard Butterfly as usual, clockwise on the left side and counterclockwise on the right side. When the loop is on the left side, make a quick about-face to the left, facing in the opposite direction—you will find yourself spinning the loop *clockwise on your right side,* thus forming the first movement of the Reverse Butterfly in front of the body. Practice this about-face until you can spin the rope easily in the clockwise direction on the right side.

Now spin the standard Butterfly and when the loop is on the right side, do a sudden about-face to the right, and you will be spinning *counterclockwise* on the *left* side.

When both of these reverse spins have been learned, it will be easy to put them together into the complete Reverse Butterfly without turning the body.

This reversal of your body position is always a good feature when giving an exhibition of vertical spinning.

Keep in mind the fact that the direction of the spin is not actually reversed in any of these movements. The loop spins in the same direction throughout, but merely appears to be different as viewed from the standpoint of the roper.

THE ROLLING BUTTERFLY

Rope—fourteen feet long with a light honda.

This flourish is a graceful variation of the standard Butterfly. Start the Butterfly back and forth in front of the body, but instead of drawing the hand directly across, draw it upward to the line of the neck, then lower it to the usual level on the other side. The loop will follow the hand and its course will form a sort of figure-of-eight. Care must be taken not to jerk the loop or force it with sudden movements.

THE ZIGZAG

Rope—fourteen feet long with a light honda.

The Zigzag is a Butterfly in which the loop is spun once on each side rather than twice. It is a favorite of the ropers and is much used in spinning exhibitions.

In this trick the loop is not carried back and forth across the body but rather is shifted in similar fashion on either side of the spinning hand which remains directly in front of the body. Thus we have the loop spinning in two parallel planes only a few inches apart, one on the left side of the spinning hand and the other on the right.

There are two methods of spinning the Zigzag, which really constitutes two separate tricks, but they are so nearly alike in effect that none but an expert can detect the difference. Both should be learned, however, and one leads easily to the other.

First, spin it exactly like the Butterfly but with one spin on each side rather than two. Give the loop a clockwise spin on the left side, and just as the honda reaches its lowest point give it a gentle pull upward and to the right which will shift the loop to the right

FIGURE 32. THE
ZIGZAG

side of the hand; then shift it back on its first revolution, making the pull as the honda reaches its lowest point. The arm remains stationary directly in front of the body, the hand turning from side to side by a movement of the waist only. This trick will take an agile and flexible wrist.

The second method differs from this in that the loop is not shifted from one side of the hand to the other, but rather the *hand is shifted* from one side of the loop to the other and the loop remains in practically the same plane throughout. If Figure 32 will be studied carefully, it will give the idea more clearly than words can do. Use a very short spoke. Make a clockwise spin just as in starting the Butterfly but with the loop directly in front of the body. In making this spin the hand is on the right side of the loop. When the spoke reaches the *top* of the loop, turn the hand over to the left and give it the second spin from the left side. Then when the spoke reaches the top again, carry the hand over the top to the right and give it another spin. There is one spin on each side, the hand turning over from one side to the other as indicated in Figure 32. The time to shift in this trick is when the spoke reaches its highest point.

If the first method of doing the Zigzag, the Butterfly method, is practiced conscientiously, you will find yourself drifting into this second method easily and naturally.

The Zigzag is an excellent climax for a series of Butterfly spins. One can go from the Butterfly to the Zigzag and back again at will.

Reverse Zigzag.—To start a Reverse Zigzag, begin by doing the Reverse Butterfly, and from there go into the Zigzag.

THE OCEAN WAVE

Rope—twenty-five feet long with a medium-heavy honda.

No trick in the whole category of roping carries more of brilliance than the Ocean Wave, save only the Skip. And the Skip and Ocean Wave are very similar, in fact, are often combined in the best presentation of the Ocean Wave. The two are frequently referred to as variations of the same trick. Ropers generally have a fondness for the Ocean Wave and at the same time regard it as one of the most difficult of roping tricks.

The Ocean Wave is really an oversized Butterfly that is carried all the way around the body. It is the Skip minus the jumping-through feature, the large loop being carried across in front of the body and then back across in the rear of the body. A clockwise spin about five-and-a-half feet in diameter is started on the right side and is carried over to the left side just as in the Butterfly, from which point it is carried back behind the left shoulder, then across the back to the right side again.

With this general description let us attack the details of learning the trick. Use a twenty-five foot rope with a medium-heavy honda. The ordinary, light honda made by bending the end back and wiring it will not supply weight enough to carry the large loop in the vertical position. On the other hand, the brass honda on the skip rope is much too heavy. Add a little weight to the

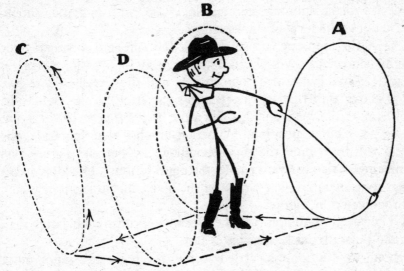

FIGURE 33. THE OCEAN WAVE, SHOWING THE SERIES OF SPINS

light honda by wrapping it with wire, or use a light aluminum honda.

Prerequisite to the learning of this trick is the mastery of the Butterfly, the Reverse Butterfly, and the Skip.

There are several ways of starting this spin but happily the method approved by tradition for exhibitions is also the easiest for the beginner. Grip the rope three feet from the end with the right hand, allowing the end to extend over into the left hand. Start the spin just as in the Butterfly with a clockwise spin on the left side, and carry it across to the right side as in the Butterfly, then back to the left side again. At this point do an about-face as in the Reverse Butterfly and the loop will be spinning clockwise on the right side and thus in position to start the Ocean Wave.

The time to pull the loop across to the left side is when the honda is at the top, that is, when it is at the twelve-o'clock position —the time is the same as in drawing the loop from right to left in the Skip. As in the Skip, the right hand must be carried across rather close to the body and must follow an upward slant to raise the loop higher on the left side. When the loop reaches the left side it will be spinning counterclockwise, and its center should be about at the level of the left shoulder.

Give the loop one full spin on the left side and then carry the right hand back over the head, thus drawing the loop straight back. After it has made one spin behind the left shoulder, give it a strong pull that carries it across the back to the right side. The time to make this pull is when the honda is at its lowest point —the six-o'clock position. When it reaches the right side, the loop will be behind the right shoulder, and here it is given one spin and carried forward to the starting position. The loop makes four spins in making the circuit of the body, the positions of which are indicated in Figure 33.

The speed of spinning in the Ocean Wave is much faster than in the Butterfly, at least twice as fast.

Similarly the loop is carried around the body at a much more brisk pace than it is moved in the Butterfly.

In the Ocean Wave the loop floats along with graceful, undulating curves. It is this characteristic movement that gives it its name.

OCEAN WAVE WITH SKIP

Rope—twenty-five feet long with a medium-heavy honda.

In this variation of the Ocean Wave, the trick is started just as in the standard Ocean Wave. Give the large loop a clockwise spin on the right side and carry it across in front of the body to the left side. Now, instead of carrying it behind the back, jump through it as in skipping, thus bringing it over to the right side,

where the trick is started over. When the loop is on the left side
it is spinning counterclockwise and is in exactly the same position
for the jump from left to right as in the standard Skip.

FORWARD-AND-BACKWARD OCEAN WAVE

Rope—twenty-five feet long with a medium-heavy honda.

This is the same as the Forward-and-Backward Butterfly except
that the rope is carried all the way around the body. Use a loop
about five feet in diameter. Start a Forward and Backward Butterfly on the right side. When the loop comes forward carry it
straight across to the left, in a plane parallel to the chest. Here
give it one spin and then carry it across behind the back in a plane
parallel to the back. All movements and timing are as in the
Forward-and-Backward Butterfly.

The only difference between this trick and the standard Ocean
Wave is in the direction that the loops face.

THE ROLLS

Rope—fourteen feet long with a light honda.

The Rolls are exceedingly difficult tricks. Being intricate and
involving a small loop, they do not carry well and possess but
little show value. Spectators very seldom realize their difficulty
or appreciate the great amount of time required to develop the
necessary skill. They receive no applause comparable to the
"hand" given the heavy tricks. Consequently many ropers feel
that they are not worth the effort required to learn them. Certainly they should not be taken up until after all the standard
roping tricks are well in hand, for the reason of their difficulty,
their lack of show value, and their inability to provide exercise
while practicing.

In the Rolls, the loop is caused to roll over the arm, the back
of the neck, the leg, or other parts of the body. In these
maneuvers, the loop is not spun from the center as in other tricks,
but rather it is given a circular jerk so that it rolls along much like
a hoop, the spoke being pulled outside the loop.

There is almost a limitless number of Rolls. Once the principle involved has been mastered, one finds himself originating new varieties constantly. This chapter will discuss a few of the better known ones which will serve to indicate the type. Since a person will be rather expert as a roper before taking up the Rolls, there will be no need to go into minute detail in describing these maneuvers.

Roll Over the Spinning Arm.—The Rolls always develop out of a Butterfly. Start a Forward-and-Backward Butterfly at the right side of the body. When the loop is thrown forward, it will be spinning in a clockwise direction. Carry this clockwise spin across in front of the body parallel to the chest in two revolutions. When it reaches the left side it should be about waist high. Give the loop one more spin and just as the honda reaches its lowest point and is ready to start upward, raise the loop upward sharply. Shove the right hand under the loop, bending the wrist up so that the hand can follow the spoke as the loop rolls over the arm. As it crosses the arm, the honda should be on the top side of the loop. As soon as the loop falls from the arm, the right hand is pulled back and picks up the spin again.

Roll Over the Shoulders.—The start of this Roll is exactly like the Roll Over the Spinning Arm described above. When the loop reaches the left side, it is lifted and pulled back onto the left shoulder. At the same time the roper bends down and the loop is rolled across his back at the line of his shoulders.

Roll Over the Chest.—This is exactly like the Roll Over the Shoulders except that the roper leans well backward and the loop is rolled across his chest.

Roll Over the Left Leg.—In this trick the left leg is extended straight out in front. The trick is started just as in the Roll Over the Spinning Arm. When the clockwise loop is carried to the left it goes under the raised leg. The right hand gives it its momentum to go back over the top of the leg from beneath it. As soon as the right hand tosses the loop up and over the leg, it releases the spoke and catches it when the loop falls on the other side.

CHAPTER IV

Trick Knots with a Lariat

With a flip of his skillful wrist the circus cowboy throws a knot into his lariat—perhaps a Pretzel, perhaps a Figure-of-eight, or perchance a Slip Knot. And it all happens so quickly as to defy the eye to detect the method. A straight rope, a flash of the wrist—and there it is! Another jerk and it is no longer there but has been transformed into another knot.

This tying of knots in the cowboy fashion takes on the flavor of magic, so deftly and quickly is it done. And with the use of one hand only! The hand is always quicker than the eye—happily so, for if it were not this way, the tying of cowboy knots would lose its glamour. These are simple knots, but when tied in the trick way they intrigue and arouse wonder—they have show value sufficient to hold a spot in any roping act. In stage roping they are sure-fire.

There is no question about the interest these cowboy knots carry for the doer. There are few more fascinating things in roping. Requiring very little muscular effort, they can be practiced during breathing spells while learning the rope-spinning tricks. These knots are well worth all the effort required for the learning. Few do them, even among the expert performers. In fact a number of the knots are original with the author.

Some of these knots belong in a rope-spinning act, being done with a spinning rope, while others fit better into a lariat-throwing exhibition, performed as they are with a catch-rope.

GRADED LIST OF TRICK KNOTS

It is recommended that the trick cowboy knots be learned in the following order:

1. Pretzel
2. Figure-of-eight
3. Overhand
4. Slip
5. Pretzel to Figure-of-eight

6. Figure-of-eight to Pretzel
7. Combinations of Knots
8. Half-hitches
9. Flying Overhand

TRICK KNOTS WITH A SPINNING ROPE

These knots are tied with the end of an ordinary spinning rope made of braided cotton sash cord. A well broken-in rope that is soft, flexible, and free from wiry kinks is required. The skip rope with its brass honda is preferred for these knots in that the weight of the honda is a decided asset. They can be done with any spinning rope, however.

THE PRETZEL

The Pretzel is the most interesting and attractive of all the knots, and since it is no more difficult than the rest, it may as well be tackled first. The fact is that when you have learned the Pretzel you have really learned how to tie two knots, and have mastered the essential features of all of them. The others are all variations of the same movement.

Take hold of your spinning rope with your right hand about three feet from the honda and allow it to hang down by your side as shown in A, Figure 34. Note that the palm of the hand as it holds the rope is up. Now quickly flip the hand over, throwing the rope back over the wrist, forming the loop shown in B. After this movement is made, the palm of the hand is down. Practice this movement many times, without attempting to complete the trick, until you can do it easily and smoothly, making a loop of the same size each time.

This done, we are ready for the second half of the trick. In the same motion with which you turn your wrist over, jerk up the honda and catch it in the loop as indicated by the arrow in B, Figure 34. Shake the loop off your wrist gently and let it fall— you will have the Pretzel shown in C, Figure 34.

Practice this trick until you can do it like a flash. It cheapens the stunt to do it slowly and deliberately. The whole idea here is to flash the knot into the rope so quickly that the eye cannot detect what happens. With practice it can be done just that quickly.

To speed up the process, as soon as you jerk up the honda shove the hand down to meet it, thus catching it in the loop. Instantly jerk the hand up again and the knot is tied.

Keep the left hand far over to the left side so that there can

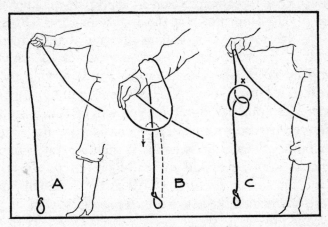

FIGURE 34. THE PRETZEL

be no question about the knot being tied by the right hand alone, entirely without assistance.

You may be surprised to find that even though you follow these instructions to the letter you get not the Pretzel, but the Figure-of-eight. There is no mystery here because the two knots are tied by exactly the same process, and this being the case, the instructions for the Figure-of-eight should be studied while learning the Pretzel.

THE FIGURE-OF-EIGHT

If you have practiced tying the Pretzel you have probably already discovered that the Figure-of-eight results from the process about as often as does the Pretzel. The beginner, therefore, jumps to the conclusion that there is no way to predict just which knot will result. On this point he is not so far wrong in that the method of tying the two knots is precisely the same, and even an expert sometimes starts to tie a Pretzel and finishes with a Figure-of-eight, much to his annoyance.

The difference rests not in the tying but in the shaking of the rope off the arm. Figure 34 shows the process of tying the Figure-of-eight as well as the Pretzel, and the instructions for the Pretzel in the foregoing section all apply. If the knot is given a jerk as it falls from the arm the Figure-of-eight (Figure 35) will result, whereas if it is shaken off gently the Pretzel will appear. If a rope with a brass honda is used, the Figure-of-eight will normally result, the weight of the honda serving to jerk it sufficiently as it falls. An unweighted honda will usually produce a Pretzel. With practice, however, you will be able to tie whichever knot you choose with reasonable consistency, using the same rope for both. Since a brass honda is such a great convenience in tying trick knots, it should always be preferred. In tying the Pretzel with it, lower the hand a little as the rope falls, thus relieving the jerk which the heavy honda produces.

Practice is the whole secret in these trick knots. You do not have a knot learned unless you can do it twenty-five or fifty times in succession without a miss on several successive days. And remember that speed is the goal for which you must aim constantly.

FROM PRETZEL TO FIGURE-OF-EIGHT

This and the trick that follows are two of the cleverest turns that can be given to the tying of trick knots with a lariat. These two tricks are original—I have never seen or heard of them being done by others in the past. Many are the stage artists of roping who tie the Pretzel and the Figure-of-eight, but I have never seen one turn a Pretzel into a Figure-of-eight by a jerk of the rope, or vice versa.

There are three parts to a knot: the knot proper, the end, and the standing part. The end refers to the end of the rope at the honda. The standing part is the section between the hand and the knot.

To get the idea of the trick, use the hand to convert the Pretzel into a Figure-of-eight: tie the Pretzel as described above, then take hold of the upper loop (X in C, Figure 34) with your left hand and turn it downward. The result is a Figure-of-eight.

Now do it in trick fashion: when the Pretzel is tied and held as in C, Figure 34, jerk the hand quickly downward so as to throw the standing part against the upper loop of the knot at X. Note in C that the standing part passes behind the upper loop of the knot. With the knot in this position, the hand would be jerked diagonally forward and downward in order to turn the upper loop downward.

In the actual tying of the knot the Pretzel should be turned so that the upper loop is toward the body and the standing part away from the body. Then the hand is jerked diagonally backward and downward. Only a slight jerk is necessary, the hand moving only about three inches, but it must be a sudden and decisive jerk.

FIGURE 35. THE FIGURE-OF-EIGHT

This is good stuff. The onlookers will label the performer as a sort of magician. It has just one shortcoming from the standpoint of showmanship—it happens so quickly that the spectators often do not realize what is happening and frequently are not aware that the resulting knot is any different from the original. To overcome this, it is well to call their attention to the change. Having tied the Pretzel, hold it up and say, "The Pretzel!—Now watch it very carefully." Convert it quickly and hold up the Figure-of-eight, saying, "The Figure-of-eight! Now let's do it again—first the Pretzel—now—it's the Figure-of-eight"!

In tying these knots before spectators, it is necessary to tie each two or three times in succession. First tie the Pretzel two or three times, then the Figure-of-eight a time or two. Then tie the Pretzel and convert it into the Figure-of-eight. Having repeated this a time or two, tie the Figure-of-eight and convert it into a Pretzel.

Practice for speed always in making these transfers. If done slowly, there is no stunt value in it.

FROM FIGURE-OF-EIGHT TO PRETZEL

This trick is performed exactly like the above. If the upper loop of the Figure-of-eight is turned downward the knot becomes a Pretzel.

Note in Figure 35 that the standing part passes behind the upper loop of the knot. By jerking the hand diagonally downward and forward, the standing part would turn the upper loop downward and thus convert the Figure-of-eight into a Pretzel. In preparing to perform the trick, it is more convenient if the knot is turned so that the standing part is away from you and the upper loop toward you. Then a slight jerk backward and downward, sharply administered, is all that is necessary.

Remember that speed is the byword always.

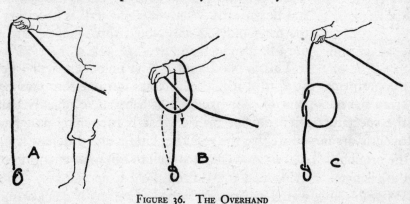

FIGURE 36. THE OVERHAND

THE OVERHAND

Figure 36 tells the story of how the Overhand Knot is done in circus fashion. Hold the rope as in A and turn the hand over, throwing the rope over the wrist as in B—this is exactly the same movement made in starting the Pretzel. At the same time that this is done, jerk up the honda and catch it in the loop as indicated by the arrow in B. When the rope is shaken off the arm, it will contain the Overhand Knot shown in C.

Note that the only respect in which the tying of this knot differs from that of the Pretzel is that the honda is passed through the loop from the opposite side—compare Figure 34 with Figure 36.

In the finished performance that comes with practice, the honda is not tossed upward through the loop as would be supposed from the arrow in B, but rather, it is jerked up only a few inches and then the hand is shot down quickly to catch it in the loop.

Practice until you can do it like a flash.

THE SLIP KNOT

This is the knot to use as the finale for the knot-tying section of a roping exhibition. I have never seen this knot tied by the ropers, and if it has been used by others in the past, I am not aware of the fact.

The method of tying is a variation of that used in the Overhand, and consequently the Overhand must be learned first. Start to tie the Overhand and as you jerk the end up to catch it in the loop, quickly shove the standing part held in the left hand in back of the end. Then complete the tying of the Overhand. When you shake the rope off your arm you will have the Slip Knot shown in B, Figure 37.

The position of the standing part in the left hand is shown in A, Figure 37—it has been shoved behind the end. Note in B, Figure 36, that in tying the Overhand this standing part is in front of the end.

It will be seen that two hands are really used in tying the Slip Knot, but the function of the left hand is so slight that it is seldom noticed. If the left hand is moved quickly the eye will not detect the part it plays. To further cover up this movement, the left hand can be placed in position before the knot is started and the left arm made rigid, then when the time arrives the body is bent downward slightly so as to give the rigid arm the movement necessary to carry the rope back to the end. This gives the impression that the roper is merely intent on making his right-hand movements correctly.

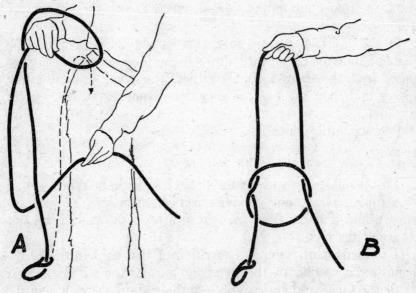

FIGURE 37. THE SLIP KNOT

COMBINATION OF KNOTS

It is possible to tie one of these knots on top of another and so produce a knot that is ornate, complicated, and impressive. In some case the result is a tangle of rope that defies description but it is always graceful in lines and the tying is spectacular and gives the impression of difficulty.

Double Overhand.—Tie an Overhand in the trick fashion described above, then immediately tie another with the same rope. The second knot forms on top of the first producing a neat and attractive tie.

Needless to say the second knot is more difficult than the first because of the presence of the first knot in the rope. Having tied the first knot, it is usually necessary for the performer to slip the right hand up a few inches, thus lengthening the rope.

Double Pretzel.—Tie the Pretzel as usual and then immediately follow with another Pretzel tied in the same way. The resulting knot forms a spread of several inches. The first knot tied, jerk the rope to make the knot smaller, then lengthen the rope slightly by slipping the hand up a few inches to provide enough length for the second knot. This maneuver requires a flexible rope that can be easily handled.

Double Figure-of-Eight.—The procedure is just as described for the Double Pretzel—tie one Figure-of-eight and follow with another in the same rope. The product is a tangle of rope that defies description but is attractive nevertheless.

Overhand and Pretzel.—Tie the Overhand and then tie the Pretzel on top of it.

Overhand and Figure-of-Eight.—Tie the Overhand and follow immediately with the Figure-of-Eight.

TRICK KNOTS WITH A CATCH-ROPE

These knots and hitches are tied with a catch-lariat rather than a spinning rope. They belong to an exhibition of lassoing rather than rope spinning. Any flexible catch-rope will serve the purpose.

THE FLYING OVERHAND

This stunt consists of throwing an Overhand Knot into the far end of a lariat twenty or thirty feet long by jerking the end through a loop.

Holding one end of the rope, toss it out on the ground so that it is lying straight and free from kinks. Now jerk the end toward you so that it rises at least a foot from the ground. Instantly after you do this, throw an overhand half-hitch down the rope through which the end should pass if it is still extended up in the air. Allow plenty of slack in the rope for the loop of the half-hitch.

The half-hitch is made by throwing the hand straight forward —this forms a loop which travels down the length of the rope and extends upward from the rope. The loop thus thrown is called an overhand half-hitch, the word *overhand* referring to the fact that the loop extends upward from the rope and is made by an overhand motion of the arm.

If the end of the rope is off the ground this loop should encircle it producing an Overhand Knot. A backward pull will tighten the knot.

This trick is difficult. On the start it will be a pure matter of luck—sometimes you will snare the end with the half-hitch, but more often the loop will miss it. It will take a great deal of practice to catch the end regularly. The feat is of no practical value, and as an exhibition of roping skill, it has less of show value than the other trick knots in this chapter.

THROWING HALF-HITCHES

Here we have a trick that not only has show value but is of great practical importance in the work-a-day life of the cowboys. It is a maneuver that every one who engages in outdoor life will find useful. In steer roping the cowboys frequently find it necessary to throw the animal and tie up his legs, and here it is the half-hitches thrown from the hand end of the lariat that ensnare the legs.

Fasten the noose of your lariat around the top of a post and stand off about ten feet. There should be plenty of slack between your hand and the post. Throw an overhand half-hitch toward the top of the post and almost at the same instant swing the hand diagonally to the left and downward. If correctly done, the half-hitch will encircle the top of the post.

The overhand half-hitch is sent down the rope by throwing the hand straight toward the top of the post as in throwing a ball. A loop will form extending upward from the rope which will roll down the length of the rope to the post. The purpose of the swing of the arm to the left and downward is to throw the loop over the top of the post—were it not for this the loop would hit the top of the post and collapse. This left swing should follow immediately after the hitch is thrown.

When you can perform the stunt at ten feet, move back a little and continue this until you can use the full length of the lariat. The farther back one stands the larger in size the half-hitches must be.

Having learned to half-hitch the top of a post, attach the noose of the lariat around the wrist of a person's arm held horizontally to the side. Throw the half-hitches in the same way, endeavoring to encircle the arm with them. With practice you will be able to rope a person and tie him up with half-hitches so that he cannot move his arms or legs.

The term *overhand* half-hitch refers to one thrown with an overhand motion of the arm—such a throw forms a loop extending upward from the rope as it moves along. The underhand half-hitch is thrown with an underhand motion of the arm and the loop thus formed extends downward from the rope.

CHAPTER V

Lariat Throwing

One can scarcely appreciate the intrigue that is coiled up in a good catch-rope until he has handled one long enough to have a feeling of mastery over it. One's rope becomes a sort of pal to him. He likes to have it near him, even though just hanging on the wall in his room, his study, or his office. It is a symbol of a rugged outdoor life, a constant reminder of joyous hours.

The lariat seems to be a sort of extension of one's self. It is a long arm that reaches out and takes hold of an object. It does no damage to its prey; it is silent, accurate, sure. It is the most personal of all the types of weapons.

The art of the catch-rope is in no wise similar to rope spinning —the equipment is not the same, the objective is different, and the movements not at all similar. Skill in one is but little help in learning the other, except for the familiarity with the general handling of ropes that results. Yet, the two arts are closely enough related so that any one who takes up one would want to learn the other.

By comparison with rope spinning, lariat throwing is much the easier to learn. True, it takes years to perfect one's skill so that he can put his rope accurately and dependably on an animal from any angle, whether the thrower is on foot or horseback, and regardless of the speed at which the animal is moving. But even so, rope spinning is unquestionably the more intricate art.

There is one form of roping that combines both rope spinning and lariat throwing—the so-called *trick-and-fancy roping* of the Wild West shows and rodeos. Here there is a preliminary display of rope spinning with the lariat which is followed immediately by a catch; that is, the spinning noose itself is hurled to rope the horse.

In the parlance of the Wild West shows and rodeos, roping is divided into three categories: *rope spinning*, in which no catch is made; *catch-roping*, in which an object is roped but without the use of spinning; and *trick-and-fancy roping*, which combines both rope spinning and catch-roping. This chapter will discuss first the art of ordinary catch-roping, and then the complicated skills of trick-and-fancy roping.

The description of the making of the proper practice rope, and of the various other types of catch-ropes useful for different purposes is recorded in Chapter I.

HANDLING THE LARIAT

There are two types of throws used in catch-roping, the *Wind-up Throw* and the *Toss*. Before approaching the subject of learning these throws, however, it is necessary that we master the art of coiling the rope and otherwise handling it skillfully. Without this ability much time will be wasted in practicing and much unnecessary confusion encountered.

COILING THE ROPE

There is a knack to coiling a rope quickly and neatly, and even though this coiling has nothing to do with the actual art of roping, it is nevertheless very important. In fact, catch-ropers and rope-spinners both are frequently judged by how neatly their ropes are coiled, both while being used and when hung up or stored away. In lariat throwing, the rope must be so neatly, carefully, and uniformly coiled that it will run out smoothly and evenly when thrown.

Take hold of the honda and toss the remainder of the rope out on the ground so that it lies reasonably straight and is free from kinks. Now form the loop and hold it in the right hand as shown in A, Figure 38. This is the loop that encircles the target when thrown. The loop should be roughly four or five feet long and should be held in the right hand at the level of the waist.

With the loop arranged, coil the remainder of the rope with the left hand as in B, Figure 38, taking the coils in the right hand.

The coils should be in the neighborhood of fifteen inches in diameter. When the rope is all coiled and held in the right hand, transfer the coils to the left hand and keep hold of the big loop only with the right hand. When transferred, the coils should be held in the left hand as illustrated in C, Figure 38—note that the

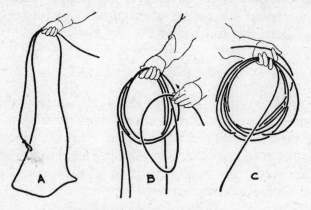

FIGURE 38. COILING THE LARIAT

end is held between the thumb and forefinger and that the three remaining fingers hold the coils.

It is of course possible and indeed often desirable to begin the coiling with the hand end of the rope rather than with the honda end. In this case, the end is held in the left hand and the coiling done with the right hand.

Ordinary coiling tends to twist the rope with the result that the coils become wiry and stand out akimbo. There is a little trick in coiling, however, which, if followed, will cause the coils to lie flat and smooth in your hand. Holding the loop in your right hand as in B, Figure 38, bring the coil around with your left hand and just as you lay it in your right hand, give it a turn toward you with the fingers of your left hand, as indicated by the arrow in B. If each coil is given this twist in the direction indicated, the twist caused by the coiling will be offset and the loop will lie flat. This should be practiced until the knack becomes so automatic that it is used unconsciously whenever rope is being coiled.

THE WIND-UP THROW

This is the type of throw in which the loop is swung around the head a few times before it is hurled at its target. It is the

FIGURE 39. THE WIND-UP THROW

type of movement that most people think of in connection with throwing a lariat.

Let us suppose that we are to rope a post three or four feet high erected in the backyard, or a chair set up on the gym or clubroom floor. Stand about ten feet from the post, facing it squarely. The proper arrangement of the rope is clearly illustrated in A, Figure 39. The loop held in the right hand is roughly three or four feet long as it hangs by the side. Note that the honda is on the *outside* of the loop, away from the body—this is important—and that it extends a little over half way down the length of the loop. The method of arranging the loop and coiling the rope is described in the preceding section.

The rope all arranged, start swinging the loop around above the head as shown in B, Figure 39. This is the wind-up and serves several purposes: It keeps the loop open constantly and ready for the throw at any instant. It gets you set for the throw —steadies your nerves, places your arm in position and readiness, and improves your control. It is the same sort of thing as a baseball pitcher's wind-up. Furthermore, it lifts the loop up off the ground and prevents it from touching any object that might deflect it, and for this reason the wind-up is an absolute necessity when roping on horseback.

The direction of the swing is from right to left—that is, as the loop is passing across in front of the body it is going from right to left. The movement is made largely with the wrist. The wrist should be relaxed, kept as flexible as possible, and you should turn the hand over (palm up) as the rope goes across behind the head, thus keeping the loop spread open and untwisted at all times. In actual roping on the range two or three swings is usually sufficient, but during one's learning days the process may be continued as long as desired. Keep the wind-up going until you are all set for the throw.

As you swing the loop overhead, its size can easily be increased. Open the hand for a fraction of a second with each swing, thus permitting a few inches of rope to slip out. The loop may be increased in this way until it feels right in the hand and seems to have the necessary size and weight to carry to the post. This ability to judge the size of the loop for a throw of any particular distance can be acquired only by experience. It will come with practice.

While winding up keep your eyes constantly on the top of the post, studying its position and judging the distance. Continue the wind-up until you are sure you know just where the post is. Then take a long step toward it with the left foot and throw the loop directly at it. Throw the whole body forward as you step, thus giving the rope momentum, using the arm chiefly to guide the loop. As you hurl the loop, open the left hand and let the coiled rope run out freely.

The whole process is similar to throwing a ball at the post with an overhand throw. Hurl the loop forward just as if you had a ball in your hand. Do not take your eyes off the post from the time the wind-up starts until the loop has hit or missed. Having released the loop, let the right arm follow through easily and naturally, keeping it up in position until the loop has reached its mark. The whole affair is really very simple, but one thing is certain, the rope will never encircle the post unless it is actually thrown there—keep your eye on the post and *put the rope there.*

If the loop fails to stay open during the wind-up, it is probably due to the fact that the rope is twisted. In this case there is no use attempting to complete the throw. Drop the rope to the ground, untwist it, and coil it up again.

From here on it is a matter of practice. Some will have better control than others, just as do some baseball pitchers. Control is largely a natural asset, but all can improve it with practice.

Count your catches as you practice. How many can you make out of fifty attempts? Do not admit that the trick is learned until you can catch the post fifty times in succession without a miss. Try to defeat your yesterday's record.

When the post can be roped regularly at ten feet, move back to fifteen, then to twenty, and so on. Thirty feet will be about the limit. Some southwestern cow-hands make catches up to forty feet but one who is dependable at thirty feet is doing plenty.

THE TOSS

In the Toss, the rope is hurled without a preliminary wind-up. The loop is merely held to the rear of the body as shown in A, Figure 40, and thrown forward as in B. The Toss is preferred by most ropers when on foot, whereas the Wind-up Throw is used almost exclusively when on horseback. On foot the Toss is as efficient as the Wind-up under all conditions except when great distance is necessary. In handling stock it is absolutely indispensable. Horses have a fear of rope and if they are subjected to roping often, they will clear away pronto at the sight of a lariat. It would be the height of folly for a roper to go into a corral swinging the loop of his lariat overhead in a wind-up—the stock would immediately be put into a frenzy and the catch made exceedingly difficult. The wise stock-hand goes in quietly, dragging the loop behind him, concealing it as much as possible, and when the opportunity presents itself, sending it forth like a flash, using the Toss rather than the Wind-up.

The loop is arranged just as in the Wind-up Throw, except that it is perhaps a little larger, there being no opportunity to enlarge it during a wind-up. Study A, Figure 40, for the details.

FIGURE 40. PREPARING FOR THE TOSS

With everything arranged swing the arm forward and upward past the side, thus sending the loop forward so that it settles down over the target. It will be noted that the movement is a sort of underhand or side-arm swing, rather than a straight overhand throw. If one is very close to the target the loop may be merely tossed forward with the arm as the roper is doing in B; however, it is usually necessary to take a long step forward with the left foot, thus swinging the body forward to give the rope momentum.

This is an easier throw to master than the Wind-up but should not be taken up until the Wind-up has been learned. Here, as in all roping, the only road to success is in untiring practice.

FIGURE 41. THE TOSS COMPLETED

THE LEFT-TO-RIGHT THROW

The post we have been using as a target extends straight up in the air and consequently can be easily roped by a right-handed person with a natural forward throw of the lariat. The same would be true if the target were a crosspiece nailed to the post so as to extend to the roper's right—a natural throw with the right hand would bring the loop in from the right so that it would easily encircle the crosspiece. This so-called natural throw with the right hand is a right-to-left throw.

The situation becomes different and much more difficult if the crosspiece extends out from the post to the roper's left. Here a backward or left-to-right throw is necessary to catch the target.

The same is true if the target is a pony's head facing to the roper's left—a backward throw would be necessary for a right-handed person, whereas if the pony faced to the roper's right, a natural or right-to-left throw would do the trick. For a left-handed person the situation is of course reversed, but for the sake of convenience we shall discuss the matter from the stand-point of a right-handed roper.

Let us assume that we are to use the Wind-up Throw to rope a target extending horizontally to the roper's left, such as a horse's head. Start the wind-up in the opposite or backward direction, that is, so that the loop, when it passes across in front of the body, is going from left to right. When the loop swings forward over the top of the head, take a long step forward with the left foot and hurl the loop forward toward the target. As it approaches the target the loop will be extending out to the left and should easily settle around it.

To use the Toss for such a catch, hold the rope a little further to the right side of the body than shown in A, Figure 40. Swing the right arm up behind the head, then forward across the top of the head, thus sending the loop forward from the left side of the body.

These Left-to-Right Throws are considerably more difficult to perform accurately and dependably than the standard type, and will take more practice.

ROPING MOVING TARGETS

The real challenge of catch-roping comes in trying to put the loop on a target that is moving. Any one with a little practice can drop the noose over a post or chair—it is easy to find and it stays there awaiting the convenience of the roper. Not so with the living agent, however, which has ideas of its own regarding the rope and the matter of being captured by it. Your steer or pony is here one second and there the next, dodging and changing pace, always heading away from the waiting noose. One has to make up his mind in a flash, and throw from all conceivable angles. It takes much in the way of skillful manipulation to catch up with such a changeable target. The Left-to-Right Throw is as essential as the standard throw, and again, the loop must often be so hurled that it will go past an animal running dead away from you and then turn and open in front of him so as to ensnare his head.

I used to practice on the horse, the cow, the dog, and even the chickens—in fact, on anything in the neighborhood that could run. Perhaps you can so train your dog that he will look upon being roped as a sort of game and enjoy it. Many dogs are like

FIGURE 42.

that. Do not attempt to rope him if he does not like it, however, for some dogs have a mortal fear of ropes and under such conditions, to throw at them would be inexcusable cruelty.

The goal of every young roper is to be able to rope a horse, yet few have horses on which to practice. A horse is not a necessity in learning the essential skills of horse catching, however, nor is one a necessity to attain the full joy of catching a running target—a boy will serve the purpose just as well.

If you will recall the horse catching by the cowboys in the circuses and the rodeos, you will note that the most spectacular catches were made by roping the animal's feet. Indeed, most of the catches in trick-and-fancy roping have as their target the legs. Sometimes it is the front legs only, and again it's all four legs. There are a few catches, however, which involve the roping of the head, the rider, or the tail.

In the tricks that follow, a good quality of maguey rope will be a decided asset (see page 16).

ROPING RUNNERS BY THE FEET

The first requirement here is for some one to play the role of the horse and run past you while you attempt to rope his feet. He should start some distance away and run past you at a space of eight or ten feet. All animals are "rope shy" at first exposure to the lariat, and the boy who runs for you will probably be no exception. That is, just as you throw for his legs he will probably shy away from you unintentionally or slow up a little to dodge the loop, thus making a good throw turn out to be a miss. To avoid this, place a stick on the ground ten feet in front of you and instruct the runner to run over it. Also tell him to run fast, pick his feet up high, and keep a constant pace, increasing his speed, if anything, as he nears the stick.

Arrange the rope in your right hand as in the ordinary Toss, but make the loop larger—it should be at least eight feet long for a beginner. Stand so that the runner comes in from your left as illustrated in A, Figure 43. Note in A that the *back* of the hand holding the loop is toward the runner. Now yell to him to come and tell him to come fast! Just as he passes throw the loop over and down toward his feet as in B, Figure 43. In B, *the back of the hand is still toward the runner*. The noose was not swung around parallel to the ground but rather thrown over and down, with the back of the hand kept toward the runner throughout. Herein lies the chief difference between roping the feet and throwing for the head—instead of throwing straight at the feet the loop is turned over and the catch made with the opposite or back side of the loop. If the throw is timed correctly, the loop will be in front of his feet as he passes and he will step into it. Then jerk up quickly and you have him. You see, he really ropes himself—all you do is throw the loop in front of him and he runs into it.

Eagerness to make the catch often tempts one to throw too soon. The time to make the cast is when the runner is directly in front of you. In fact, you can even wait until he is a few feet past you—it is always easier to make a catch when he is a little past than before he has come into line with you. When one throws too soon the loop collapses before the runner reaches it. He may catch his foot in it as it lies on the ground, but a clean roping catch is impossible.

Just as soon as you tighten the rope around his legs, drop the lariat on the ground so as not to trip him. The runner can be a great help to you in learning if he will run fast and pick his feet up high, for the faster the running the easier is the catch.

FIGURE 43. ROPING A RUNNER BY THE FEET

He can cooperate, too, by not shying, changing pace, or attempting to hurdle the noose. He must get the idea that he is not playing a game with you, attempting to prevent you from roping him, but rather, helping you by running as you direct. However, he will not fancy the task if he is tripped and thrown each time he is caught. You must cooperate with him in this respect if you expect him to cooperate with you.

If the runner is coming in from the opposite direction, that is, from your right, the throw is made in exactly the same way. In this case the palm of the rope hand would be toward the runner throughout.

When the catch can be made regularly at ten feet, increase the distance to fifteen.

This stunt of roping by the feet is great sport. It is always fun to do and is a spectacular number in any roping exhibition.

ROPING SEVERAL RUNNERS

The circus cowboy who ropes six horses running abreast in one loop is really performing a very simple feat, for it is no more difficult to rope several runners than it is one, provided they are running in line and close together. The only difference is in the size of the loop. Figure 44 illustrates the trick.

FIGURE 44. ROPING SEVERAL RUNNERS BY THE FEET

Start out by roping two boys with arms locked and running together. Proceed just as if there were only one, following all the instructions given in the preceding section on how to rope a runner by the feet. You will find the stunt in no wise different or more difficult than roping a lone runner. This accomplished, double the number and rope four runners, then six!

The important thing is that the runners lock arms and stay as close together as possible, keeping in step as they run. A line of six will of course require a very large loop—it is better to err on the side of too large a loop than too small a one, since the rope can be jerked up quickly once the runners are in it, thus taking up the slack immediately. When a big loop like this is used, the top of the loop strikes the waist line of the runners as they step into it and they are thus captured around the body instead of the ankles.

Here we have one of the most spectacular of the catch-roping stunts and consequently one that is particularly effective in a roping demonstration.

ROPING HORSES BY THE FRONT LEGS

The circus crowd is quick to acclaim the roper who catches the running horse so spectacularly, but few give a thought to the

FIGURE 45. CATCHING ALL FOUR LEGS

contribution to the act made by the rider of the horse or that made by the horse himself. The horse must be put past the proper point at the right time, without shying away or changing pace. The roper and the rider constitute a team that has practiced together repeatedly. The horse, too, comes in for consideration because some ponies are too high strung for the job and others are too "rope shy"—all the practice in the world would not make suitable performers of these. The ponies that serve as targets for the ropers' art are carefully selected, being suitable by temperament for the task, and are trained for it by long rehearsal. If the horse were running wild around the arena, the roper would have to be on horseback himself to catch him. Since the roper is expected to stand on one spot and display his skill, the horse must be ridden past him within reach.

It is necessary, therefore, that we have a suitable horse and a rider to handle him for us. If the horse is ridden past just as the boy ran past in the preceding section, it will be no more difficult to catch his front legs than it was to catch the boy, and the procedure is precisely the same. Don't shy from the horse as he comes by—step right up and throw the loop down toward his front feet. Read the preceding section on roping runners for the details. As soon as the horse hits the rope, jerk up quickly and you will have him by the front legs. Then release the lariat at once and let it fall to the ground so as not to trip him. Further, have the rider stop the horse as soon as the catch is made. If you should throw the horse you might not only hurt him and his rider, but would probably develop a fear of the rope on the part of the pony, thus making him rope shy and ruining him for the purpose thereafter. There is no danger of such a result if the lariat is dropped as soon as the legs are caught.

The rider should station himself at least fifty feet from the roper and wait until the roper calls or signals him to come. Then he should ride past at a good fast canter or trot. The catch made, the rider stops the horse and allows the rope to fall off the legs, then immediately rides back and prepares to run for the next catch.

Several horses can be caught in one big loop by following the same procedure used in roping several boys running with locked arms. The horses must be kept abreast and as close together as possible. Each horse must have a rider. Simple as it is for any good roper, this feat always proves to be most dramatic.

CATCHING ALL FOUR LEGS

Shake out a large loop and throw it in front of the approaching horses' feet in the usual way. After the horse hits the rope, hesitate for a second or so, then jerk up the rope—you should have him by all four legs. If you jerk up immediately, the rope will close on his front legs, but by hesitating a second the hind legs will have time to enter the loop. The horse should canter, not trot. Release the rope immediately after the catch has been made.

ROPING THE HORSE'S NECK

The horse should be ridden past the roper in the usual manner at a distance away from him of about fifteen feet. Either the Wind-up Throw or the Toss may be used. The technique of the throw is the same as if a post were being roped. A small loop should be used, three or four feet in diameter. Wait until the horse's head is directly opposite you, then toss the loop straight out and over his neck. Do not throw until the horse is opposite or, if anything, a little past you. If you can rope a post you will find this catch very simple indeed.

ROPING BOTH HORSE AND RIDER

In this stunt the loop of the lariat is caused to encircle both the horse's head and the rider. The throw is made in exactly the same way as when roping a horse by the head, except that a larger loop is used. Throw the loop high enough so that the lower rope catches the horse under the jaw, thus permitting the upper rope of the loop to settle down behind the rider's back. The motion of the running horse aids in carrying the rider into the loop. Jerk up the loop as soon as the catch is made.

CATCHING THE HORSE'S TAIL

Here is a stunt that brings a laugh always. It is a favorite of the circus clowns who mimic the feats of the cowboys while they are roping, although it is often used by the ropers themselves.

The horse should be stationed to your right and ridden past you in the usual way. Use a very small loop, not more than two feet in diameter. Step up close to the horse as he approaches, and just after he has passed you, slap the loop up sharply onto his rump and around his tail. The rider should ride right on after the catch, dragging the lariat after him. Let out rope after the catch until the limit has been reached, then hang on to the end and run along after the horse, pulling on the rope in an apparent effort to stop him.

ROPING WHILE STANDING ON YOUR HEAD

This spectacular feat is done by a few of the better stunt-ropers and is occasionally seen in the rodeos. It consists of roping a horse by the feet while standing on your head. For a gymnasium exhibition, a boy will serve as well as a horse. The two prerequisites are, first, the ability to catch a horse or runner by the feet, and second, the ability to stand on your head steadily with the aid of the left hand only.

Draw a line on the ground on which you are to do the head stand. Arrange a large loop and lay it out carefully on the ground behind the line, with the part to be held by the hand extending up to the line. The right hand is to hold the loop at this point while you are standing on your head. Lay the coils of the lariat in front of the line at the point where the left hand is to be, keeping the end only in the left hand. Now stand on your head, facing away from the spot the horse is to cross, taking the weight on your head and left hand. As soon as you have everything under control, yell to the rider to come. Just as the horse passes, throw the loop forward toward his feet, with the right hand,.thus causing the horse to step into it. Since the rope is lying on the ground it will uncoil of its own accord.

Since you are facing away from the horse it is impossible to see him at the time of the throw. From rehearsal with the rider, however, you know the distance away from you that the horse will pass. You can tell from the sound of his hoofs when he is passing you, but it will be better to have the rider yell when the proper second arrives for the throw.

At best this stunt will take much practice and long rehearsal with the rider.

THROWING THE LARIAT WITH THE FOOT

In this trick the loop is hurled forward with the right foot instead of the hand. The object is to catch the runner around the head. Shake out a large loop as for the Toss and lay it on the ground. Let go of it with the right hand and place the toe of the right foot under the point where the hand was. Place the left foot well forward. As the runner approaches kick the right foot forward and upward vigorously, thus causing the loop to open up and fly forward in the same way as if it were thrown by the hand.

TRICK-AND-FANCY ROPING

The expression "trick-and-fancy roping" refers to a combination of rope spinning and catch-roping; it involves a preliminary display of rope spinning while the horse is approaching which is terminated by a catch of the horse as he passes. Such roping always involves a catch at the end, otherwise it would be merely rope spinning. Without the preliminary display of spinning, the stunt would be called ordinary catch-roping.

While any of the rope-spinning tricks may be used in the preliminary flourish of spinning, yet almost invariably the choice of the ropers is the Ocean Wave. Trick-and-fancy roping, therefore, really refers to an Ocean Wave which terminates with a catch. Since it involves the best of rope-spinning ability (the Ocean Wave being one of the hardest of the tricks) and the best of catch-roping skill, trick-and-fancy roping represents the acme of roping performance.

Although some show cowboys do a trick-and-fancy roping turn while sitting on horseback, practically all such roping is done on foot. A thoroughly skilled and dependable rider is necessary to bring the horse past at precisely the right second in order that he will be within reach when the spinning rope is in the proper position.

Before one can attempt this feat he must be a thorough master of the intricacies of the Ocean Wave.

A good quality of maguey rope of the proper size and weight to suit the roper is required (see page 16). It is well to use this rope in practicing the Ocean Wave in order to lay the proper foundation for the trick catching.

THE OCEAN-WAVE CATCH

Mark out the path down which the rider is to canter the horse. Stand about ten feet from this path with your right side toward it and facing in the direction from which the horse is coming. Start the Ocean Wave as usual and when the loop passes your back let it go right on over to the right until it crosses the path. A great deal of practice of this movement will be necessary before one is ready to practice with the horse and rider.

This much learned, it is a case of perfect coöperation and timing between the rope and the rider. Long practice will determine just how far away the horse must be to reach the roper at the proper second, and also how many times the Ocean Wave must be carried around the body while the horse is covering a certain distance and coming within roping range.

As the horse comes up, carry the Ocean Wave around the body, pull the loop across the back briskly and let it continue on over in front of the horse. As the loop approaches the horse's path, pull back slightly on the rope in order to turn the loop at right angles to the path so that the horse can step into it.

Any of the standard catches described earlier in this chapter may be made in this way: catching the front feet, all four legs, the horse's head, and both horse and rider.

Many variations in the use of the Ocean Wave in this connection may be worked out. For example, the roper may wait until the horse almost reaches him, then start the Ocean Wave in front, carry it around behind and then on over for the catch. Or he may carry the Ocean Wave around him three or four times before throwing for the catch. Again he may insert one or more

Skips in the series. Each one of these tricks must be worked out with the rider to insure the proper timing.

THE ROLLING CATCH

In this trick the loop is rolled like a hoop along the ground into the horse's path. In its simplest form, the loop is arranged as for a Flat Spin except that it is held at the right side of the body. The hand is carried over and forward, thus rolling the loop along the ground. More frequently the trick starts with an enlarged Butterfly. When the loop reaches the right side of the body, going counterclockwise, it is carried forward and down to the ground, where it is rolled into the horse's path.

Rolls of this sort are often seen in connection with the Ocean-Wave catches.

CHAPTER VI

Roping Exhibitions and Contests

Every one who learns to rope wants to display his ability to others. He hopes some day to be able to do a complete and finished roping act of the type performed by the artists of the stage. Organizations using roping as an activity usually feature it in demonstrations, field days, shows, parents' nights, and so forth. In fact, one of the most appealing aspects of roping is its show value—folks like to watch it. It is unique, different, colorful; its symbolism stirs imagination; it is graceful, esthetic, pleasing to the eye.

This chapter presents the routines for individual roping acts and for mass demonstrations. It describes certain special stunts that add color to roping shows.

When roping is used in organizations such as clubs, camps, playgrounds, and gymnasiums, the ropers welcome contests which test ability and determine champions. The last half of this chapter is devoted to such roping championships and contests, and to games involving roping.

ROPING DEMONSTRATIONS

There is a traditional type of roping act in which the roper talks along as he ropes, getting off a quaint humor that smacks of the ranch house and a homely philosophy that reminds one of the old Westerner who finds himself, boots, hat, and all, on Fifth Avenue in New York. Good ropers use such comedy in a quiet, casual sort of way, if at all, merely to add a little sparkle to their roping, but they rely chiefly on the roping itself to "get across." Some actors who are better comedians than ropers, use the roping solely as a screen for their comedy.

There are other ropers who do their roping turn as best they can, going at it in business-like fashion, and say nothing at all during the course of the act. Such is the characteristic way of real, honest-to-goodness, ranch-raised ropers who work in the rodeos. This is by all means the course to follow unless one has marked talent as a comedian. There will be sufficient glamour and appeal in the roping to insure success for a short, fast, rope-spinning act without resorting to the addition of comedy. This proves to be the case in rodeos, circuses, and the like, the talking type of act being limited to the theater stage. In a gymnasium exhibition, a playground demonstration, or a camp circus, to attempt to talk would be a mistake—the thing to do is to concentrate on good roping. The same would apply to a stage roping act put on by any one who is not most gifted in comedy.

In roping before an audience the emphasis should always be on graceful, rhythmic movement. One's desire to impress often leads to speeding up the spinning in an effort to make it appear more spectacular. Invariably the resulting effect is the very opposite of that desired. The charm of rope spinning rests in the beauty of the graceful, floating curves of the rope. When one gets down to the finale with its Big Loops, Hurdles, and Skips, then is the time for speed and strenuous effort, but not so with the lighter tricks which constitute the body of the act.

ONE-MAN ROPE-SPINNING ACT

Much depends on the order in which the various tricks are presented in a roping act. It is a fundamental principle of showmanship that the least difficult and impressive stunts should be used at the start and the series should gradually build up to the stronger ones, closing always with the most spectacular.

While the following order of tricks is presented with this principle of showmanship in mind, it should be remembered that it is suggestive merely, and could be nothing more than such, since roping tricks vary in spectacular qualities as different ropers do them. One will find from experience which of his tricks are the most striking. On one point there will be no dispute, however—the large, heavy-rope tricks are more colorful than the light-rope ones. For example, a good roping act can be put on without even including the delicate and difficult Butterflies and Rolls, provided it makes skillful use of the less intricate but heavier tricks. This being the case, the flashy Skips and Hurdles should always be used as concluding features. It is not the difficulty of the trick that determines its spot in the act, but rather its spectacular qualities.

The following recommended order of tricks assumes that one can do all of the tricks in these chapters. Such a complete array is, of course, not necessary for a good demonstration. The general order will apply, however, regardless of how many tricks are to be included.

The tricks should be presented in approximately the following order:

1. *Trick Knots*

   Overhand
   Pretzel
   Figure-of-eight
   Pretzel to Figure-of-eight
   Figure-of-eight to Pretzel
   Double Overhand
   Slip Knot

2. *Flat Spins with Twenty-Foot Rope*

   Wedding Ring
   Hand-shaking
   Juggle
   Lying down

3. *Flat Spins with Sixteen-Foot Rope*

   Flat Spin
   Merry-go-round
   Two-handed Merry-go-round
   Jumping into Flat Loop
   Jumping Out
   Up and Over

Juggling Up and Over
Lift onto Body
Skyrocket
Tapping In and Out

4. *Vertical Spins with Sixteen-Foot Rope*

Butterfly
Forward-and-backward Butterfly
Arrowhead
Vertical Raise onto Arm
Rolling Butterfly
Zigzag

5. *Flat Spins with Twenty-five-Foot Rope, Brass Honda*

Hand-shaking around One Leg
Hand-shaking around Alternate Legs
Hurdling

6. *Flat Spin with Seventy-five-Foot Rope, Very Heavy Honda*

Big Loop

7. *Vertical Spins with Twenty-five-Foot Rope*

Ocean Wave

8. *Vertical Spins with Twenty-five-Foot Rope, Brass Honda*

Skip
Skip and Turn

It will be noted that the demonstration is broken up into units, each unit consisting of a series of tricks which calls for a different rope than the preceding. Some ropers have argued that the mark of good roping is the ability to do practically all tricks with the same rope. Suffice it to say that such ropers do not do a wide variety of tricks since it would be absolutely impossible to perform all the tricks listed above with the same rope. More than anything else, the thing that makes the difference in ropes is the weight of the hondas. Sections 2, 3, and 4 in the above list might be done with the same rope, but even here the chances are that the roper will have a special rope for each of these series which he will prefer to use. It would be stupid not to use the rope best suited for each trick. When the series of tricks with one rope is finished, that rope should be coiled up and placed aside as the next rope is picked up.

The series of tricks using the same rope should be done continuously, without hesitation between the tricks. That is, the roper should go from one trick to another without allowing the spinning loop to stop. This will not always be possible but it will be in many cases.

Five to six minutes is a good length for a roping act. It requires a whale of a good act, no matter what it consists of, to carry longer than six minutes.

PARTNERS IN ROPING

An effective roping act may be presented by two people roping together, each sharing the spot equally. This is frequently done by a boy and a girl. In presenting the simpler tricks, both may be roping at the same time, standing side by side, the purpose being to present a spectacle of gracefully floating ropes. In handling the more spectacular tricks, however, the ropers should take turns.

There are a few tricks in which both may work in the same rope. For example, the two may stand close together while one spins a Wedding Ring around them both. After a few spins the other may take the spoke without stopping the spin and continue it. The spoke may thus be passed back and forth frequently. The Wedding Ring may then be turned into a Juggle and this followed by Hand-shaking. In the latter trick the roper on the right, spinning the rope with his right hand, drops the loop to the floor, and the one on the left takes the end in his left hand and carries it around behind, where the first roper takes it in his right hand and brings it around in front again, and so on.

One of the best of the partner tricks is the Skip. The two stand one behind the other, as close together as possible, the one doing the roping standing in front. The Skip is performed in the usual fashion with the partners jumping together and thus both skipping the rope. This requires long practice.

Occasionally a man will present his roping act with a lady assisting him by handing up the various ropes as he needs them. When the finale is reached with its Skip, the girl joins the roper in the partner trick and both skip together.

MASS ROPING EXHIBITIONS

No more beautiful sight can be presented in a gymnasium than fifty ropers, spaced uniformly about the floor, all spinning their ropes at the same time. This eclipses completely any of the traditional mass demonstrations of gymnastic exercises. So, too, on the playground, or the campus of the summer camp—mass roping, wherever staged, has excellent show value. Furthermore, as a gym or playground demonstration feature it has the valuable asset of presenting all the individuals who are able to rope, not merely the few star performers.

The main requirement for a successful mass demonstration is that all ropers perform the same trick at the same time. It is not necessary that all arms and ropes move in unison—that would be scarcely possible nor would it be desirable—but all should be doing the same trick. This means that the possibilities are limited to a few simple tricks that all can do perfectly. The picture is destroyed if a few of the ropes are breaking down constantly, which would be the case if difficult tricks were being attempted.

This necessity of using simple tricks in no wise detracts from the effectiveness of the exhibition, for the reason that it is gracefully floating ropes that create the desired mass picture, and here there is nothing more satisfying than the Wedding Ring. No more could be asked for than a floor covered with beautiful, smooth, rhythmic Wedding Rings. A slow Juggle is another good trick, provided all are able to do it well, which, unfortunately, will seldom be the case. The Merry-go-round has no superior for mass use. In short, the Wedding Ring and the Merry-go-round are the two ideal tricks and it is unwise to attempt to go farther than these. Indeed, the Merry-go-round may be eliminated if need be, thus letting the Wedding Ring stand alone.

It should be emphasized to the ropers that the objective is a mass picture, and consequently all individual frills and flourishes should be eliminated.

If it is desired to present as many ropers as possible and at the same time as many different tricks as possible, all in one number, the procedure to follow is to form a mass chorus of ropers across the floor, all doing the Wedding Ring, and place a star performer in front on one side, facing the stands, which latter does the complete series of roping tricks. If the crowd is on both sides of the arena or floor, a star performer may be placed on each side. All the time the ropers occupying these spots are performing, the chorus ropers continue to do a steady, rhythmic Wedding Ring.

AN AMATEUR CATCH-ROPING ACT

Horses suitable for roping will scarcely be available in the field days and exhibitions put on by physical-education departments, camps, clubs, and playgrounds, and neither will the persons in such demonstrations be familiar with such roping, with the result that the usual pattern for a catch-roping act cannot be followed. This fact, however, will not prevent the inclusion of a good lariat-throwing act in such a program whether it be staged in a gymnasium or out-of-doors.

A stationary object can be placed in the center of the arena or floor to serve as a target. A gym horse makes a very acceptable object for the reason that when one faces its side there is an extension both at the right end and left end, thus making possible both right-to-left and left-to-right throws. Minus such a horse, a chair, box or any similar object may be used.

A boy may be used as a running target with catches made around both his head and feet. Six or eight boys with arms locked will make possible the big catches. A boy riding a bicycle will supply a fast-moving target.

Each catch should be demonstrated three times in succession before taking up the next one.

The order of events may be as follows:

Stationary Target

> Wind-up Throw
> Toss
> Backward (Left-to-right) Wind-up Throw
> Backward (Left-to-right) Toss
> Half-hitches

Running Target

> Toss for Head
> Wind-up Throw for Head
> Throw for feet
> Catching Two Runners at Once
> Catching Eight Runners at Once

Bicycle Target

> Toss for Rider from Standing Position
> Wind-up Throw for Rider from Standing Position
> Wind-up Throw for Rider while Riding Bicycle

A HORSE-ROPING ACT

A horse trained for roping and an expert rider will be necessary for a standard catch-roping exhibition. The following tricks should be included in such an act:

> Toss for Horse's Head
> Wind-up Throw for Horse's Head
> Throw for Front Feet
> Throw for All Four Legs
> Throw for Both Horse and Rider
> Throw for Horse's Tail

GYMNASIUM ROPING EXHIBITION

These suggestions for a roping exhibition in a gymnasium or similar inclosed area apply to physical-education demonstrations,

Boy Scout rallies, Y.M.C.A. open houses, and all similar events in which roping may fit into the program.

The traditional physical-education exhibition with its more or less formal presentation of exercises, tumbling, acrobatics, and dancing is giving way to a pageant-like approach with much emphasis on color. The ideal procedure here is to assume a theme and then use the traditional activities, giving them the color suggested by the theme. A few special activities growing out of the theme will be used also. Such a demonstration not only presents all the usual activities but sets them forth in such a way that they carry a romantic touch and thus appeal strongly to imagination. This is simply good showmanship—good showmanship for the type of activities the physical-education department is sponsoring.

A theme may be selected that is appropriate to the section of the country in which the city is located, using the color characteristic of the area, although this is not at all necessary, and is difficult to do, year in and year out, and still be original. There are many excellent themes, offering remarkable opportunities for color, that are always appealing wherever they may be staged —and the old-time West is one of these.

Entirely aside from its use in such demonstrations based on Western atmosphere, roping will make a colorful spot in any exhibition or rally.

The roping may all be thrown into one number or it may be divided into the following several acts, each carrying punch enough to stand alone:

> Catch-Roping of Stationary Targets
> Mass Rope Spinning
> Catch-Roping of Running Boys
> Catch-Roping of Bicycle Riders
> Rope-Spinning Act (by two or three stars)
> Whip Cracking

SPECIAL DEMONSTRATION STUNTS

Here are a few special stunts—frills, if you please—which may be used to add a colorful and dramatic touch to a roping demonstration.

COLORED STREAMERS

Hold a strip of red, yellow, or blue silk of very light weight, two to three feet long, in the left hand. Spin the Wedding Ring as usual, and when it is going nicely, throw the strip of cloth

FIGURE 46. WAVING THE FLAG

against the spoke as it comes around in front. The streamer will float out behind the spoke as it encircles the body.

Two or three streamers of different colors may be kept in the pocket and pulled out and thrown on one at a time, thus placing two or three floating colors on the spoke. They should be spaced equally, one above the other. It is more effective if the streamers are of unequal length.

Another method equally as effective is to tie a number of streamers to the rope at distances apart of two feet, this being done before the spinning starts. By handling the rope carefully, this will not interfere in any way with starting the spin.

WAVING THE FLAG

Attach a small American flag about a foot in length to the spoke of a twenty-foot rope and proceed to spin the Wedding Ring—the flag will float beautifully behind the spoke as it swings around the body. Figure 46 shows it. For the best effect, the flag should be attached so that the bottom is about a foot above the point where the honda rests in spinning.

A special rope that is not needed in the other stunts should be used for this feature. The flag should be attached before the exhibition starts and the rope coiled up in the usual way. It can then be picked up and spun without hesitation when the time arrives.

LIGHTED ROPES

Attach a small electric light bulb just below the honda of a twenty-foot rope and run the wire along the rope to the battery held in the hand at the rope's end. Start to spin the Wedding Ring as usual and after a moment of spinning have all lights turned off, leaving the place in darkness. After a few seconds of darkness, light the bulb on the rope. The effect is vivid and beautiful.

Three bulbs may be attached instead of one—one at the honda, one across the loop from the honda, and one midway between the honda and the hand.

A still more colorful effect can be produced by using bulbs of varying colors resembling a string of Christmas-tree lights.

LUMINOUS ROPES

Another delightful feature on a darkened stage is produced by painting the ropes with luminous paint. This creates an entirely different scene from that produced by electric bulbs attached to the rope. The painted rope flickers softly and beautifully.

In staging this scene it is well to have two or three ropers with luminous ropes standing on the lighted stage. The orchestra should play softly and slowly some old-time western tune. After a moment of spinning on the lighted stage, the lights should be faded out slowly into complete blackness, leaving visible only the flickering ropes.

DANCING IN A ROPE

Such a trick as the Wedding Ring leaves the entire body free and unencumbered for dancing, and practically every movement in the usual tap-dancing routine can be done without the rope interfering with the dancing. With practice most of the flat spins and such light verticals as the Butterflies can be done while dancing. The most effective maneuvers, however, are those in which the dancer is inside of the spinning loop most of the time. It is possible to step in and out of a flat spin without breaking the rhythm of the dancing.

A good finale to a combined dancing and roping act is the trick called Tapping In and Out, described on page 54.

I know of one stunt enthusiast who dances, spins the Wedding Ring with his left hand, and plays a trumpet with his right, all at the same time.

ROPING CHAMPIONSHIPS

In organizations for girls and boys in which roping is featured, the roping championships are always enjoyed and looked forward to with much anticipation. The rope-spinning championship of a summer camp is always a much-sought-after honor. Likewise on a playground or in a Scout troop. Perhaps the most definite means of stimulating the ropers to perfect and polish their skills is the knowledge that they will soon match skills with the others in the championship contest.

ROPE-SPINNING CONTEST

Because of the nature of the activity there is no way to conduct a rope-spinning championship contest other than to base the rating of the contestants upon the opinions of a group of judges. Appoint a panel of three judges, one at least being a person familiar with all the intricacies of good roping. The ropers should be called upon to display their skill in two series of tricks, one the flat spins and the other the vertical spins. Prepare two lists of tricks, one containing the flat tricks such as those listed on page 22 , and the other the verticals recorded on page 65. Place these lists in the hands of both the contestants and the judges some time before the event.

The ropers need not present their tricks in the order on the list, the list merely serving to indicate to them the events the judges will anticipate and which they will consider as an indication of complete performance.

The names of the contestants should be thrown into a hat and then pulled one at a time to determine the order in which the ropers will compete. Each roper in turn performs all the tricks on the list that he is able to do and any others not on the list. The judges watch the demonstrations and grade each roper on each trick.

The selection of the winners is based upon the following items in good roping: (1) number of tricks performed, (2) technical correctness of the tricks, (3) grace of movement, (4) rhythm, (5) showmanship. The most satisfactory procedure is to grade each trick on the basis of these items and then total the grades for the contestant's score. In a contest made up of ropers of average skill, such as would be the case in a camp, club, or playground, greater weight should be given the vertical spins as compared to the average run of flat spins. The usual procedure is to double the ordinary rating in order to obtain the score for the vertical spins and for the more difficult flat spins such as the Lift onto Body and the Skyrocket. The scores made in the other flat spins are added to these doubled scores to determine the contestant's total rating.

As an added precaution, it is well for the judges to select the three contestants with the highest rating and have them compete a second time in order better to rate them as first, second, and third. In this second performance the judges can give more careful attention to rhythm, grace, and showmanship.

LARIAT-THROWING CONTEST—STATIONARY TARGET

The contestants may use any type of lariat they choose. Since they take turns in competing, the same rope may be passed around if necessary.

One or more of four types of contest may be used here: (1) *Most Consecutive Throws, Number 1*; (2) *Most Consecutive Throws, Number 2*; (3) *Throwing Half-hitches*; (4) *Longest Throw*. The first of these is the one most commonly used.

Most Consecutive Throws, Number 1.—Place a post, chair, or other object to serve as a target fifteen to twenty feet from a throwing line, the exact distance depending on the skill of the contestants. The players take turns in competing. Each makes twenty-five throws from behind the throwing line and is credited with one point each time the loop of the lariat completely encircles the target. Either the Wind-Up Throw or the Toss may be used as the contestant prefers. The contestant wins that makes the highest score.

Most Consecutive Throws, Number 2.—The target consists of a post five feet high on the top of which a six-foot bar has been nailed so that it extends three feet out to each side. The throwing line should be fifteen to twenty feet distant, parallel to the crossbar. The contestants take turns in competing, each making ten throws of the standard type with a right-to-left swing of the arm (for a right-handed player), and ten more throws of the opposite or left-to-right type. Each successful catch scores one point. The one with the highest score wins.

Throwing Half-hitches.—The target is the same as in the preceding contest, and the throwing line is ten to fifteen feet distant. The contestants take turns in competing. The contestant throws and catches the crossbar and then makes five attempts to throw a half-hitch around the bar. He makes five of these throws, each being followed by five attempts at half-hitches. One point is scored for each successful half-hitch. The one with the highest score wins.

Longest Throw.—Mark a series of throwing lines ten, fifteen, twenty, twenty-five, and thirty feet out from the target. Each contestant makes three throws from the ten-foot mark, three from the fifteen-foot mark, and so on. He scores one point for each successful throw from the ten-foot line, two points for each from the fifteen-point line, three from the twenty-foot line, four from the twenty-five foot line, and five from the thirty-foot line. The player with the highest score wins.

LARIAT-THROWING CONTEST—MOVING TARGET

Mark a throwing line on the ground and ten feet from it and parallel to it, another line known as the target line. The moving target may be either a running boy, a boy riding a bicycle, or a horse.

Running-Boy Target.—The runner stands fifty feet from the roper. At the roper's signal, he runs down the target line and the roper attempts to rope him as he passes. He has ten attempts and scores one point for each successful catch. If, in the judges' estimation, the runner changes pace or dodges away from the rope, the attempt is played over. The contestant with the highest score wins.

Two contests are possible here—roping the runner by the feet and roping him by the head. The first is preferable.

Bicycle Target.—This contest is the same as the above except that the target consists of a person riding a bicycle and the aim is to rope him over the head.

Running-Horse Target.—This event is conducted in the same way as roping the running boy. There must be a rider for the horse who puts him past the roper at the proper time and distance. The rider must control the horse so as to give each roper a fair chance in each attempt; otherwise the attempt is repeated.

Two contests are possible—roping the horse by the head and by the feet. The latter is always more popular and should be preferred.

LARIAT-THROWING CONTEST WHILE MOUNTED

Most organizations will not possess horses trained for roping but that need not rule out the event—the roper may ride a bicycle. This makes an excellent contest for a playground or a gymnasium.

Erect a post or other object for a target and mark a throwing line ten to fifteen feet away, the distance depending on the skill of the contestants.

Roping from a Bicycle.—The roper rides down the throwing line and attempts to rope the post as he passes. The contestants take turns in competing. It will usually require twenty-five throws to determine a winner, in that if fewer throws are required there will be many ties. One point is scored for each successful catch and the person with the highest score wins.

Roping from a Horse.—The conditions are the same as in roping from a bicycle except that a horse is ridden.

ROPING GAMES AND CONTESTS

Here are a few roping games and contests that will be much enjoyed by boys and girls for informal sport around a club, camp, playground, or gymnasium. Since most of these call for no more in the way of roping skill than the Wedding Ring, or a simple throw with a lariat, a beginner has as much chance as the expert and all enjoy them equally.

ROPE-SPINNING DUEL

This is a dual contest and is an excellent council-ring event.* The two ropers, standing a few feet apart, start to spin the Wedding Ring, and at the starting signal attack each other with intent to stop the opponent's rope from spinning. The one wins who stops his opponent's rope provided his own rope is still spinning. All tactics are fair.

* For a detailed description of how a council-ring program of dual contests is conducted, and a description of many suitable events, see Bernard S. Mason and E. D. Mitchell, *Social Games for Recreation*, pages 223 to 292. New York: A. S. Barnes & Company, 1935.

As soon as one of the pair is defeated, some one challenges the winner, and this continues until all have competed and the champion has thus been determined.

Variation.—Same as the above except that the Flat Loop is spun instead of the Wedding Ring.

MASS ROPING FIGHT

This event is similar to the Rope-spinning Duel except that several players are competing at once. All start to spin the Wedding Ring and at the signal all attempt to stop the others' ropes from spinning. The one wins whose rope is spinning after all the others' have been stopped. An area should be marked out beyond the boundaries of which the ropers cannot retreat. Stepping over the boundary eliminates the offender.

CATCH-ROPING DUEL

While scarcely usable in the confines of a council ring, this dual contest is interesting to boys on the campus, playground, and gym floor. Mark out an area about fifty feet square within which the two players must remain. Each player has a catch-rope. At the signal both try to rope the other and at the same time to avoid being roped. The one wins who first closes the noose of his rope tightly on the other. Some one challenges the winner and so the contest continues until a champion is determined.

FREE-FOR-ALL CATCH-ROPING

This is the same as the Catch-roping Duel except that several are competing at once, each trying to rope the others and to avoid being roped. As soon as a player is roped he is eliminated and withdraws. The one wins who remains when all others have been roped. An area should be marked out within which the players must remain.

WEDDING-RING RACE

The distance is fifty yards. Each holding his spinning rope, the contestants line up behind the starting line, so spread out that there are at least eight feet between the individual players. All start to spin the Wedding Ring and when all have it going, the starting signal is given. The contestants run down the course while spinning the rope and the one wins who finishes first provided his rope is still spinning. A contestant is eliminated the moment his rope ceases to spin.

Flat-Loop Race.—This is like the Wedding-ring Race except that the Flat Loop is spun and the distance is twenty-five yards.

WEDDING-RING BICYCLE RACE

This event is the same as the Wedding-ring Race except that the contestants ride bicycles. The distance is one hundred yards. Each contestant places one leg over the bicycle preparatory to mounting, and while in this position starts the Wedding Ring. The starting signal is given when all ropes are spinning.

LARIAT RACE

Establish a starting line and parallel to it mark four other lines, all lines being fifteen feet apart. Mark a spot on the starting line for each contestant, these spots being ten feet apart. Out from each of these spots on each fifteen-foot stripe, drive a stake two feet high into the ground. Thus there is a row of four stakes in front of each contestant as he stands on the starting line, these stakes being fifteen feet apart. Each contestant has a catch-rope.

At the signal each player tries to rope the nearest stake. He is not permitted to step over the starting line until the stake is "caught." Once the stake is roped, he runs to it, removes the lariat, and tries to rope the next stake. This continues until the last stake is roped, whereupon the contestant runs to it to finish. The one finishing first wins.

SKIPPING RACE

This difficult event is suitable only for expert ropers. The distance is twenty-five yards. The racers go down the distance with the Running Skip (see page 72). The one finishing first wins.

CALF-ROPING CONTEST

This is a standard event of the western rodeos and while it can scarcely be used by amateurs in other settings, it will be of interest to all ropers nevertheless.

The calf is enclosed in a pen and the roper, mounted on his horse, is stationed behind a line about twenty-five feet in back of the gate to the pen. The gate is opened and when the calf runs out the referee blows his whistle and the roper dashes in pursuit. He ropes the calf with his catch-rope, leaps from his horse and runs up to him, touching him with his hand. The timers record the time with a stop-watch from the whistle until the hand is placed on the calf. Then the next contestant tries, using another calf. The one with the best time wins.

Sometimes this event is conducted by requiring the roper to place a rubber band around the calf's lower jaw. Having done this he throws up his hands as the signal to the timers.

BULLDOGGING

The colorful event to which western tradition has attached the name of Bulldogging involves no roping at all, and certainly it is no pastime for amateurs, being a dangerous and daring undertaking when attempted by even the most experienced and hardened of professionals. On two counts, therefore, it does not fall within the strict scope of this chapter. However, every one concerned with learning to rope will be interested in knowing the events associated with roping in the rodeos and the rules governing them. Certainly he will want to be able to talk the language of the rodeos and "Bulldogging" is an important word in that language.

Rather than roping his steer with his lariat, the bulldogger seizes him by the horns with his hands and wrestles him to the ground. He chases the steer on his horse and when near enough, dives down grasping the horns with his hands, stops the steer's progress by bracing the feet of his stiffened legs against the ground, then throws the steer by wrenching his horns. Needless to say it is a strenuous and rugged sport, replete with hazard at every turn.

INDEX